AF632637

FUNCTIONAL FAMILIES

AS I SEE IT

Verses Kindler Publication

Verses Kindler Publication.

Website: www.verseskindlerpublication.com

Functional Families As I see it

By: Ms. Antar Anger

ISBN: 978-93-5605-344-1

NON-FICTION STORIES 1st Edition

Price: INR 350/ $18

Disclaimer

Functional families as I see it is written by Antar Anger.

The published work is the original contents of the author and she has done her best to edit and make it plagiarism-free.

The characters may be fictitious or based on real events but they are not meant to hurt anyone's feelings nor portray anything against any caste or system. Any resemblance of names of actual person, place or institute is purely coincidental to carry forward the story.

In case of any plagiarized write-up, the author is solely responsible for it, the publisher would not be responsible for it.

Table of Content

Chapter 1 - The Power of Play

Beneath a canopy of lush vegetation, the Petersons' suburban home sat contentedly as morning broke over the peaceful cul-de-sac. A calm background was created by the quiet rustle of leaves in the breeze and the soft buzz of morning birds. The tidy rows of homes, each with a welcoming porch and well-kept lawns, gave off an air of elegance. A well-travelled trail wound through the community, beckoning early risers to stroll under the street's row of trees. This gorgeous corner of the earth promised peace before a busy day, and the morning was no exception. The soft twitter of awaking birds was heard all over.

The family comprised the ever-diligent mother, Sarah who was the coordinator of the household. The father, Michael, whose mornings were a blur of emails and coffee; and their two sons, Ben, 7, and Ethan, 9. They brought a mixture of enthusiasm and mischief to the beginning of each day.

By 6:30 AM, the Peterson home was alive with the sounds of waking life. Sarah's alarm would gently chime at 5:30 AM, and she would always be the first to rise. She loved spending time by herself. She liked enjoying her first cup of coffee while everyone else was still asleep. She cooked a daily cycle of oatmeal, scrambled eggs, and pancakes for breakfast, making sure there was something for everyone according to their taste.

Michael usually rolled out of bed by 6:15 AM, groggy but alert enough to fumble for his phone. He checked overnight emails from his team in different time zones while the scent of freshly brewed coffee guided him to the kitchen. By 6:45 AM, he was usually dressed and ready, setting the table for breakfast and pouring juice for the boys.

Ethan, the eldest, was responsible for feeding their golden retriever, Max. He loved the routine, the happy wagging of Max's tail, and the way the dog eagerly awaited his breakfast. It was a small task but one he took seriously. By 7:00 AM, Ethan was already dressed for school, his backpack neatly packed the night before.

Ben, however, was a different story. The youngest Peterson often found more interest in his father's smartphone than in his morning duties.

He was meant to be getting dressed or helping arrange the dinner, but most of the time he was discovered sitting on the floor in the living room, playing games or looking through apps on Michael's phone. His little fingers had unexpected dexterity; he could swipe and tap with the dexterity of a much older person.

"Ben, come on, buddy. We need to get moving!" Sarah called out from the kitchen, catching sight of her younger son out of the corner of her eye.

"Just a minute, Mom. I'm almost at the next level," Ben replied, eyes glued to the screen.

Michael chuckled, shaking his head. "You're too good with that thing, sport. But you know the rules—no screens before school."

Reluctantly, Ben handed over the phone and shuffled off to his room to get dressed, though not without a dramatic sigh. Ethan, meanwhile, took his place at the breakfast table, Max happily munching away at his kibble.

The house was bustling with activity by 7:30 AM. Michael made sure everyone was on time, Sarah checked backpacks and schoolwork at the last minute, and the guys finished their meal swiftly. Their mornings had a reassuring routine and a feeling of togetherness that kept everything going well, even with the odd setback.

The sun was shining brightly on the Petersons' house when they finally got into the car and prepared for the day. It was just another wonderfully imperfect morning, full of the little pleasures and difficulties that constituted their daily existence.

When Sarah Peterson came into the parking lot at 5:00 PM, she realized that she had a long day. She had been juggling between deadlines and meetings. Her job had endless demands. There was a faint chance that she could steal a few minutes of rest before she dived into her evening duties. As she approached the front door,and stepped inside she knew her hope was just her dream.

The home was a mess. School Books were abandoned on the couch, toys strewn all over the living room floor. There was the definite smell for something burnt in the air, suggesting one of her sons had made a disastrous snack attempt. Sarah looked around, her shoulders drooping.

Her tone sharpened with displeasure as she whispered under her breath, "How did they manage this in just one hour?" She glanced at the time, which read 5:05 PM.

"Ethan! Ben!" She yelled, breaking through the cacophony of the TV blasting in the background. "Get down here, now!"

Her mature nine-year-old son Ethan was the first to answer. With a glance of sheepish remorse on his face, he leaped down the stairs. "Hi, Mom. Sorry for the mess." He apologized and began gathering up and putting away a few toys.

Ben, however, was unable to be found. Sarah was aware of his whereabouts. She headed for the kitchen, where she could definitely hear someone playing a game. Her seven-year-old son was seated at the kitchen table, engrossed entirely in her phone.

"Ben," she said, her voice strained but controlled. "What did I tell you about taking my phone without asking?"

Ben didn't look up. "Just one more minute, Mom. I'm almost done with this level."

Sarah was losing patience. She went to Ben and took the phone from his hands. "Enough. This is not how you ask for permission. And look at this mess! You need to clean up with your brother."

Ben's face twisted in anger. "But I was almost there! You never let me enjoy my game!" he shouted, storming off to his room.

Sarah took a deep breath. She felt a flash of anger but quickly suppressed it. She knew reacting with anger wouldn't help the situation. She turned back to Ethan, who had been diligently tidying up.

"Thank you for helping, Ethan. I really appreciate it," she said, softening her tone.

Ethan nodded. There was a small smile on his face. "It's okay, Mom. I am there for you."

Sarah and Ethan labored together to try and restore some form of in order to the house as the clock approached 6:00 PM.

Michael entered just as they were wrapping up, appearing just as worn out from his workday. He said, "Hey, everyone," as he untied his necktie and placed his laptop bag by the entrance. "How was your day?"

"Eventful," Sarah replied with a wry smile. "The boys got home before me and, well, you can see the aftermath."

Michael chuckled and kissed Sarah on the cheek. "I'll handle dinner. You sit down for a bit."

Sarah nodded gratefully but knew her respite would be short-lived. She started setting the table while Michael whipped up something quick for dinner. The boys were called to the table, and they gathered for a meal that was more chaotic than peaceful.

Ben picked at his food, still sulking from earlier. "I'm not hungry," saying this, he pushed his plate away.

Sarah's frustration flared again. "Ben, you need to eat. You can't just skip meals because you're upset."

"I'm not hungry," Ben repeated stubbornly.

Michael intervened gently. "Buddy, you need to eat something. Just a little bit, okay?"

Ben grudgingly took a few bites but remained sullen throughout dinner. The rest of the family ate in a tense silence, broken only by Ethan's occasional attempts to lighten the mood with stories from school.

After dinner, as they cleaned up, Sarah noticed Ben inching towards Michael's phone on the kitchen counter. "Ben, no more screens tonight," she said firmly.

"But I want to watch my show," he protested.

"Not right now. You need to learn there are limits," Sarah replied, her voice firm but calm.

Anger darkened Ben's face. With a growl under his breath, he stomped off. Ethan looked at his parents, then at his brother. He said, "I'll go check on him."

Shaking his head, Michael answered, "No, let him cool off." "He has to gain an understanding that screaming and arguments will not get him what he actually wants."

An hour later, Ben had managed to grab Michael's phone again. He sat on the couch, engrossed in his game. Ethan, feeling protective of the rules, decided to intervene. "Ben, give me the phone. Mom and Dad said no more screens tonight."

"No! It's mine!" Ben shouted, clutching the phone tighter.

"Ben, come on. You're going to get in more trouble," Ethan insisted, trying to grab the phone.

As the fight escalated, the boys began pulling the phone. When Ethan finally got Ben to get go of it, Ben became furious and banged the door as he fled to his room. He re-emerged with their shared laptop and sat on his bed, furiously clicking through his favorite shows.

Michael and Sarah exchanged worried glances. "We need to talk about this," Sarah said softly.

The parents took a seat in the living room after the boys had gone to bed, feeling exhausted from the evening.

"Do you think we're being too strict with the screen time?" Michael asked, rubbing his temples.

"I don't know," Sarah admitted. "But I don't like how obsessed Ben is becoming with it. It's all he thinks about."

Michael nodded. "Maybe we need to find a better balance. Set clearer boundaries but also give him some controlled screen time. He's obviously using it to cope with something."

"I agree," Sarah said, leaning back on the couch. "It's just... I want them to enjoy other things too. To not rely on screens for entertainment or comfort."

"We'll figure it out," Michael assured her. "We'll talk to them this weekend, make a new plan. Together."

Sarah smiled, grateful for Michael's support. "Thank you. I just want what's best for them."

They turned out the lights and went to bed. They were both filled with optimism and concern about the future of their children. Parenting was a difficult path, yet they knew they would get through it together, one step at a time.

The next day unfolded much like any other in the Peterson household. The morning routine was executed with the same blend of efficiency and chaos that had become their norm.

By evening, the boys had returned from school, and Sarah had come back from work. While Michael was on his way. Pre-dinner activities, such as homework, housework, and the sound of pots and pans clattering in the kitchen, filled the house with a buzz.

The smell of baked chicken and veggies filled the air as dinnertime drew near. After setting the table, Sarah invited the guys to take a seat. But Ethan had other plans.

"Mom, can I take my plate to the living room and watch my show while I eat?" Ethan asked, his eyes hopeful.

"No, Ethan," Sarah replied firmly. "We have dinner together at the dining table. Eating on the couch is a bad habit."

Ethan's face darkened with frustration. "When I was Ben's age, you used to let me eat in front of the TV. You even turned it on for me sometimes! Wasn't that a bad habit too?"

Sarah was taken aback by Ethan's retort. Memories flashed through her mind of those evenings after a demanding day when she'd allowed Ethan to eat in front of the TV in order to keep him occupied and quiet. She had bought herself a few moments of quiet by using the television as a tool to control the mayhem. She was suddenly faced with the implications of her choices, and she was at a loss for how to react.

"Things are different now," she said weakly, but the conviction in her voice was missing.

Ethan pressed on. "It doesn't seem fair. Ben gets away with everything because he's younger, and I get punished for the same things you let him do."

Without warning, Sarah's frustration boiled over. The sound of her slap across Ethan's face echoed in the sudden silence. Ethan turned and ran to his room after giving her a startled and hurting look. Tears running down his face.

The room was heavy with silence. Ben, who had been sitting quietly with Michael's phone, placed it down and went to the dining table without a word, afraid to provoke any further conflict. Sarah stood in the kitchen, her hand still trembling from the outburst.
Michael had just entered and witnessed the confrontation come to a conclusion. He knew that he had to take charge of the situation and release the tension. He moved to Ethan's room and gave it a small knock before going in.

"Ethan, can I come in?" he asked softly.

With his face hidden in his pillow, Ethan lay on his bed. Ethan didn't respond. Michael entered the room taking his silence as permission. He sat down beside him.

"Hey, buddy," Michael said in a soft voice. "I am aware of your anger. Mom didn't mean to harm you at all. When we're angry, we occasionally say or do things and later regret it."

With tears still rolling out from his eyes, Ethan slightly turned his head. "Daddy, it's not fair. Mom and you always warn us against using our phones or watching too much TV, yet you still do it."

Michael nodded, acknowledging the truth in Ethan's words. "You're right. We do use our phones and watch TV, sometimes more than we should. And maybe we haven't been the best at setting a good example. But rules are important because they help us make better choices."

Ethan sat up, wiping his eyes. "It just feels like the rules change all the time."

Michael wrapped his youngster in a reassuring arm. "I understand that it appears that way, but our goal is to act in your and Ben's best interests. Alright, let's talk about it together. But let's have dinner first, for now."

Ethan nodded reluctantly, and they made their way inside to the dining room. When family members sat down to dine, there was no conversation at all. The only noises were the clink of silverware and Ben's occasional murmurs.

After dinner, the boys went to their rooms, leaving Michael and Sarah to clean up. They moved around the kitchen in silence, each lost in their thoughts. Finally, Sarah spoke up.

"I lost control," she said quietly. "I shouldn't have hit him."

Michael placed a hand on her shoulder. "We both need to do better. We set rules, but we're inconsistent with them. We use TV and gadgets when it suits us, and then we're surprised when the boys want to do the same."

Sarah leaning over the counter said, "I recall the times when I was so exhausted that I had to let Ethan watch TV while he ate in order to keep him calm.

"Now we see the consequences," Michael finished. "We need to find a balance. We can't use screens as a crutch and expect the boys to follow rules we don't stick to ourselves."

They sat down together, the weight of their mistakes heavy on their shoulders.

They talked late into the night. They thought of coming up with a fresh strategy to control screen time and establish more clear boundaries. they chose to include them in the conversation and decision-making process.
This was an attempt to make the boys feel more responsible and less resentful.

The next morning, they called Ben and Ethan in the living room. The boys appeared nervous, not knowing what to expect.

"We need to talk," Michael began. "Last night didn't go well, and that's on us as much as it is on you."

Sarah nodded. "We haven't been fair or consistent with the rules about screen time. We've used it as a quick fix, and that's not right. We want to make a new plan together, so it works for all of us."

Ethan looked at his parents, still hurt but willing to listen. "What kind of plan?"

"We'll set specific times for when you can use the TV or phones," Michael explained. "And we'll follow those rules too. But we'll also find other things to do as a family, like games or outdoor activities. We want to spend more time with you, not just rely on screens to keep you occupied."

Ben, sensing the seriousness of the discussion, nodded. "Okay. But can we still watch our favorite shows sometimes?"

"Yes, Ben," Sarah said with a smile. "But we'll all stick to the rules, even us. And we'll make sure we're spending quality time together, not just staring at screens."
The boys agreed. The family was all set to go and proceed to implement their new strategy the rest of the day. TIt wasn't perfect. There were still moments when temptation and annoyance found their way. Yet, there was also a new sense of togetherness.

That night, as the boys went to bed, Sarah and Michael sat in the living room, feeling hopeful for the first time in a while.

"It'll take time," Michael said, taking Sarah's hand. "But we're on the right track."

Sarah squeezed his hand. "We are. And we'll get through this together."
"Parenting is never an easy journey, but we know that we can overcome the obstacles ahead through honest communication and an open mind to learn from our mistakes." Michael said.

Sarah and Michael went into their bed room to discuss how they could improve their family's routine. They wanted to create more meaningful connections and reduce their reliance on screens. Sarah took a deep breath, determined to find a better balance.

"I think we should start our day differently," Sarah began.
"I normally wake up at five in the morning. We can use the additional hours for something special if I can do the most of the day's cooking and preparation before the boys get up."

Michael nodded thoughtfully. "That's a great idea. What if we ask the boys to get up just 15 minutes earlier than usual? We could take them out for a morning walk. It would be a great way to start the day, get some fresh air, and spend quality time together."

"I like that," Sarah agreed. "And in the evenings, we can focus on outdoor activities. We could start with simple things like playing badminton or football in the backyard. It'll be good for all of us to get some exercise and have fun."

"How about we plan some bigger activities for the weekends?" Michael suggested. "We could go fishing on Saturdays. The boys would love it, and it would give us a chance to unwind and bond in nature."

"That sounds perfect," Sarah said with a smile. "We could also have a monthly picnic. It doesn't have to be anything elaborate—just pack some food and head to a local park. It'll be a nice change of pace."

****

The more they talked, the more ideas came in. They decided to include riding bikes through the neighborhood, going to the nearby swimming pool and going on hikes in the surrounding area. They even thought of teaching the boys some fundamental gardening skills so they could plant and maintain their own small backyard patches.

As they drew out their plans, they understood they had to sure that such activities were a regular part of their routine. They made a plan that struck a balance between work, school, and play.

Like usual, Sarah woke up around five the following morning. With a goal, she made breakfast and started working on dinner in the kitchen. By 6:30 AM, she had done most of the day's cooking. Feeling accomplished, she went upstairs to wake the boys.

She gently nudged them awake and whispered, "Ethan, Ben, it's time to get up. We are heading for a stroll this morning."

The boys complained a little yet jumped out of bed. They were curious by this break from the routine. The family left the house around 7:00 AM, walking across the neighborhood invigorated by the crisp morning air. As they watched the early morning light peeking through the trees and spotting the birds they thought about the success of their plan.

The backyard became alive with the sounds of sport and laughter in the evenings. Ben and Ethan took turns playing badminton with their parents. They kept encouraging each other as the shuttlecock zipped back and forth. On other days, as they tossed a football about, their happy shouts echoed in the evening air.

Fishing outings were scheduled for Saturday mornings. The boys learned from Michael how to cast their lines and wait patiently for a bite.

The peaceful surroundings and shared excitement of catching fish created cherished memories. The boys loved the thrill of reeling in their catches, and the quiet moments by the water allowed the family to connect on a deeper level.

On one sunny Saturday each month, the Petersons would take a basket of food and head to a local park. They spread out their mats under a shady tree. Then they ate homemade sandwiches, fruit, and Sarah's delicious cookies. Sarah and Michael watched the boys contentedly as they ran around, played tag, and explored the playground.

The new routine brought a noticeable change to the family dynamic. The boys enthusiastically got involved in the activities, eagerly awaiting their sports in the evening and their walks in the morning. The time spent outdoors not only improved theeir family's relationship but also their physical health.

Developing positive routines was crucial for developing positive habits. The Petersons discovered that they could cut down on the boys' time on screens without making it feel like a punishment by establishing a regular timetable. The guys, on the other hand, regarded it as a chance to partake in enjoyable, worthwhile activities.

Morning walks became a staple, helping the boys start their day with energy and positivity. The fresh air and light exercise made them more alert and ready for school. Evenings filled with outdoor games gave them a chance to burn off energy, making bedtime smoother and more peaceful.

By incorporating these pursuits into their everyday routines, Sarah and Michael exemplified the value of moderation and balance. They demonstrated to the boys that although entertainment might be found on screens, true happiness and contentment had come from spending time with each other and exploring their surroundings.

These routines also instilled a sense of responsibility and teamwork. The boys learned to help with preparations for picnics, take care of their garden patches, and contribute to family activities. This not only built their confidence but also taught them valuable life skills.

Sarah and Micheal had seen how the screen time had affected their children.The growth and wellbeing of their children was greatly impacted by excessive television viewing. Cognitively, it resulted in attention issues that made it challenging for them to focus on work and achieve academic success. Their attention spans shortened and their capacity to deeply connect with instructional material reduced by the constant onslaught of fast-paced images and information.

Long-term TV watching promoted sedentary behavior, which increases the risk of obesity by lowering physical activity and exposing viewers to commercials for unhealthy foods.

They knew that the blue light emitted by screens would disrupt sleep cycles. This can worsen sleep disorders that further impair cognitive abilities and general health. Too much TV viewing can socially and emotionally stifle possibilities for in-person interactions, which are essential for fostering emotional intelligence and effective communication.

Furthermore, exposure to unsuitable content might have a detrimental effect on values and conduct. Consequently, excessive television use had a number of hazards, making it imperative for children's holistic development to maintain a balance between media intake and active lifestyle choices. Television can serve as an educational tool when utilized carefully and wisely.The growth and wellbeing of a child can be greatly impacted by television consumption. Mentally, it

But after changing their way of life, the Petersons saw a marked improvement in their family's general well-being as the weeks went by. The boys had a revitalized sense of belonging and affection as a result of spending quality time together, and they were more content and involved. They had effectively set the stage for better habits and a closer family tie by developing and adhering to these routines.

The Petersons had realized how important it was to develop excellent habits. They came to understand that habits form the basis of everyday existence and have an impact on everything from emotional health to productivity. In a world when chaos and overwhelm are commonplace, having good routines brings order and regularity. Once formed, habits need less conscious effort and become nearly automatic, which frees up mental space for other crucial activities and decisions, as Sarah and Michael were aware of. They recognized that consistent activities result in sustainable behaviors, which led them to create positive routines for their family.

Their new strategy was centered around planned weekend events, games in the evenings, and walks in the morning. The Petersons realized the power of strong habits. They understood that routines shape daily life, influencing emotional well-being and productivity. In a world filled with chaos, structured routines provide stability. Over time, good habits become automatic, allowing more mental space for meaningful activities. This realization motivated Sarah and Michael to establish positive family routines.

Chapter 2 - The Family Potluck

The Petersons' house was in the centre of a thriving, multicultural neighbourhood. It exemplified the value of variety. This suburban sanctuary was in a peaceful cul-de-sac. It was home to families from all over the world, mixing cultures together. The neighbourhood came to life with a distinct blend of sounds, sights, and scents. It looked like a beautiful blend of communal life. As the morning light rose, it covered the region in a golden glow. The Petersons' house was in the centre.

The houses that lined the street all had similar suburban styles. Yet they also all had the heritage of their owners' past. The Petersons' house had a tidy front yard and inviting garden. The Chatterjees, who immigrated to America from India only two years ago. They are their neighbors to the left. They came here as Mr Chatterjee had received an interesting job offer from an American company.

Their house had a well-kept garden full of vivid jasmine and marigolds, whose scents mixed with the cool morning air. Their house served as a striking display of their Indian heritage's rich culture. They often shared their love for their homeland through lively Diwali celebrations. Along with decorating their home, they would light up the street with laughter and lights. On festive occasions, the aroma of delicious Indian delicacies would spread in the air.

Mr Chatterjee was a prominent gentleman from Bengal. He had a profound love for classical music. He had always been mesmerized by the melodies of the sitar and the complex rhythms of the tabla. The strains of Rabindra Sangeet frequently filled his nights. Evoking a sentimental and culturally rich mood. Often, the sound of their kids practising the tabla and sitar filled the air. This added to the soothing melody of the neighbourhood's early morning.

He was married to Arpita, a beautiful Brahmin girl with serene, expressive eyes and a gentle demeanour. Arpita's grace and traditional values were reflected in her devotion to vegetarianism, a lifestyle she embraced with pride. She often wore elegant saris, her hair neatly tied back, embodying the timeless beauty of her heritage.

Although Arpita was a strict vegetarian and Mr. Chatterjee was a gourmet of fish and meat, their relationship thrived on mutual respect and love despite their different dietary habits. They made sure both of their tastes were respected in their shared kitchen by tactfully managing their culinary differences.

The Chatterjee enhanced the neighbourhood's multicultural tapestry by introducing the Petersons to the rich flavours of Bengali food and the evocative notes of classical music. Their story is a blend of traditions with new beginnings in a foreign land. It represents the elegance of cross-cultural communication and harmony.

The Petersons' neighbours welcomed them with smiles as they went outside for their daily walk. The grass had dew on it that gleamed like small diamonds as the sun had just started to peak over the horizon. The light was warm and golden. The neighbourhood's distinct identity is attributed to the harmonious blend of various cultural influences present in the air.
Michael and Sarah walked hand in hand and enjoyed the peacefulness of the early morning. Ben and Ethan ran ahead. Their laughter made the quiet street resound. They waved at Mrs Chatterjee, who was watering her plants.

The neighbourhood was diverse not only because of the various cultures that coexisted there. It was also because of the ways in which these cultures blended together to improve the quality of life for all who called it home. Frequently, the Petersons discovered fresh information from their neighbours, be it a customary event, a new dish, or an alternative viewpoint. The neighbourhood is now a true mixture of international customs and friendships. This cultural interchange also promoted a strong feeling of community and respect for one another.

Ethan and Ben were able to grow up in a rich environment because of the lively blending of cultures. Their perspectives were expanded and profound. This taught them to appreciate diversity. It got ingrained in them as a result of being exposed to a world of customs, languages, and cuisines.

Their neighbourhood was more a community than just a place to live in.
It was a community that celebrated both individuality and togetherness. A community that embraced the beauty of diversity and the strength of unity. It was the perfect place to raise their family. It was a perfect place to teach their children the values of acceptance, respect, and love for all cultures.

The Petersons were excited to spread the holiday spirit throughout their ethnic neighbourhood. They were looking forward to organizing their potluck this coming weekend. With lists in hand, Michael and Sarah sat down at the kitchen table to discuss possible meal items for their get-together. Ethan and Ben, the lads, could not contain their excitement for the celebrations that were coming up, so they darted around.

Sarah added, "Let's make this potluck extra special," her eyes shining with excitement. "We would request the Chatterjees' to bring a dish from their culture. It will be a lovely way to honour our multicultural community."

Michael nodded in agreement. "That's a fantastic idea! I can't wait to see what everyone brings."

Micheal picked up the phone and called Mr Chatterjee. His conversation was filled with excitement and warmth. When he called the Chatterjees, Mrs. Chatterjee answered the call cheerfully, "Hello, Michael! Merry Christmas!"

"Merry Christmas, Mrs. Chatterjee! We're planning to host a potluck. We would love you to join us. We were thinking it would be wonderful if you brought a dish from your culture. What do you think?" Sarah asked, her voice filled with enthusiasm.

Mrs Chatterjee's laughter echoed through the phone. "Oh, that sounds delightful! I'd be happy to make biryani. It's a family favourite and perfect for sharing."

Sarah's heart swelled with joy. "That sounds amazing! I just can't wait to try it."

On the day of the potluck, the Petersons' home was filled with the scents. There were sounds of festive preparations. Ethan and Ben helped with the decoration. Their excitement grew with each passing hour. The house was filled with the smells of freshly baked cookies and roasting turkey. The aroma of pine from the Christmas tree blended with it.

The neighbours were amazed to see the Petersons' home. The house was transformed into a vibrant, multicultural celebration. The Chatterjees entered with a large pot of fragrant biryani. The aroma of its spices filled the air with warmth. Mrs Chatterjee had also prepared

Rasagulla, a sweet dish that the Bengalis relish. She beamed as she set it down on the table, her joy evident.

That was not all. Keeping in mind the little boys, she even prepared bubbling Lasagna and a beautifully decorated panettone.

The table was a feast for the senses. It was a delightful array of colors, textures, and aromas. All that reflected the rich culture. The Petersons stood back. They admired the spread and felt a deep sense of gratitude for their diverse and loving community.

Mr Chatterjee was beaming with enthusiasm as he proudly placed the tray of fish on the table. "Ladies and gentlemen," he announced, "this fish has been cooked by yours truly, Mr Chatterjee. It's my special recipe. So, I expect everyone to give it a try. I promise it won't bite back!"

Laughter erupted around the table at his playful remark, and the enticing aroma of the fish had everyone eagerly reaching for a piece.

Laughter and talk filled the room when everybody gathered around the table. Each dish was introduced with stories and traditions, bringing everyone closer together. As they heard about the many civilizations and their distinctive celebrations, Ethan and Ben listened carefully, their eyes bright with curiosity, as they learned about the different cultures and their unique ways of celebrating.

The evening was filled with warmth, joy, and the shared appreciation of each other's heritage. The Petersons' potluck had become more than just a meal; it was a celebration of unity, diversity, and the beautiful connections that bind their community together.

As the potluck dinner progressed, Ethan and Ben found themselves chatting with the Chatterjee children, Anika and Raj. The table was laden with delicious dishes, but Anika seemed hesitant. "Why aren't you trying the chicken?" Ethan asked curiously.

Anika smiled politely. "I am a vegetarian. I don't eat meat. It's a part of our family's tradition and beliefs."

Ethan's eyes widened with interest. "Wow, that's different. So what do you usually eat?"

Anika explained, "We eat a lot of vegetables, lentils, and grains. Our mom makes amazing vegetarian dishes."

Ben chimed in, "That biryani she brought smells really good!"

Raj said, "It is! You should try it!"

As the potluck dinner continued, Ethan found himself increasingly curious about Anika vegetarian diet. He watched as she happily dug into their mom's fragrant biryani and a variety of vegetable dishes, steering clear of the meat options on the table. Ethan, his curiosity piqued, decided to ask more.

"You know, eating meat gives you a lot of important nutrients," Ethan said, picking up a piece of roasted chicken. "Like protein, iron, and vitamins. How do you get those if you don't eat meat?"

To this Mrs Chatterjee smiled, ready to explain. "We get our protein from lentils, beans, tofu, and dairy products. For example, the biryani we brought has a lot of protein from chickpeas and lentils. And we eat plenty of leafy greens and other vegetables that are rich in iron."

Raj nodded, chiming in, "Plus, we eat nuts and seeds that give us healthy fats and more protein. It's a balanced diet, just without the meat."

"Wow, Raj, you really know a lot about vegetarian nutrition," Ethan said, impressed. "But you eat non-veg, too, right?"

Raj grinned mischievously as he reached for the serving platter, placing a roasted chicken leg and a piece of fish on his plate. "Oh, I definitely do!" he said with a wink. "I like to balance my diet—lots of veggies and a little bit of this delicious 'seafood' and 'leg-tarian' cuisine!"

Everyone burst into laughter at Raj's playful take on his diverse eating habits.

Ethan listened intently. "I didn't know you could get so much from vegetables. But what about things like B12? My parents always say that's important, and I heard you can mostly get it from meat."

Anika nodded thoughtfully. "You're right. Animal sources are the best for Vitamin B12. That's why we sometimes take supplements to make sure we're getting enough. My mom is really careful about making sure our diet is balanced and nutritious."

Ethan was impressed. "That's cool. I guess there are different ways to be healthy. I love chicken, but your biryani does smell amazing. Can I try some?"

Anika beamed. "Of course! Try it with some of the raita, too. It's really tasty."

As Ethan scooped a portion of the biryani onto his plate, he realized that despite their different dietary choices, they all valued good nutrition and tasty food. The conversation highlighted the rich nutritional benefits of both their diets. Meat is a great source of high-quality protein and essential amino acids. It also provides iron and vitamins like B12. All these are crucial for growth and energy. Meanwhile, the vegetarian diet of the Chatterjees offers a variety of proteins from plant-based sources. In a vegetarian diet, you get iron from greens and legumes. The healthy fats can be obtained from nuts and seeds. All this ensures a well-rounded and nutritious intake.

As they shared and talked about their meals, they developed a mutual respect and understanding of one another's eating habits. This further enhanced the cultural richness of their get-together.

"Anika, hold on a minute," Ben remarked with a puzzled brow after giving it some thought. You just said you're vegetarian. Then what's this chickpea you're talking about? I thought 'chick' meant chicken!"

Everyone burst into laughter at Ben's confusion. Anika giggled and shook her head. "No, Ben! Chickpeas are not chickens. They're a type of legume, like beans. They're completely vegetarian."

Raj added with a grin, "Yeah, they don't go 'cluck-cluck'! They're more like 'crunch-crunch' in your biryani!"

Ben blushed but laughed along, realizing his mistake. "Oh, I get it now. Well, in that case, I'm definitely trying them!"

Mrs Chatterjee offered Lasagna to Ben. Ben, though, is well-known as a picky eater. He shook his head and wrinkled his nose. "No thanks," he muttered, suspiciously glancing at the Lasagna.

Ben and other picky eaters tend to limit their diet to a small number of well-known dishes. They avoid new or unfamiliar foods by just looking at texture or even appearance. They don't even taste these strange dishes. Mealtimes can be difficult because of this reluctance, particularly in multicultural settings where there are many different flavours and components.

On seeing Ben's hesitation, Micheal knelt down to his level and smiled warmly. "Ben, this Lasagna is very special. It is filled with delicious vegetables and a lot of cheese. It is like a tiny package of happiness."

Ben still looked unsure, so Michael continued, "You know, trying new foods can be an adventure. Just like when you try a new game or a new book. You might discover something you really like."

Mr Chatterjee joined in, "I used to be afraid of trying new foods too, Ben, when I was your age. But then I tried new dishes, and now few of them are my favorites. How about you just try one bite? I am sure you are going to like it. Yet, If you still don't like it, you don't have to eat more."

Sarah, smiling warmly, said, "Ben, I know you are unsure about the taste of Lasagna. How about this? Let's make it a fun game. Take one small bite, and if you like it, you get to tell everyone at the table how brave you were for trying something new."

Ben looked at her, intrigued by the idea. "Just one bite?" he asked.

"Just one bite," Sarah confirmed. "And remember, sometimes trying new foods may help you discover something you really like."

Ben grudgingly used his fork to take up a tiny piece of the Lasagna. He was encouraged by seeing Ethan, who was already loving it. He nibbled a little, eating intently. He was surprised to find that the flavour wasn't as weird as he had imagined. Instead, the flavours were light and nice.

A smile slowly spread across his face. "This is actually pretty good," Ben admitted, reaching for another.

Sarah beamed. "See? I knew you could do it! Sometimes, it just takes a little courage to find new favorites."
The room filled with applause and cheers, celebrating Ben's small but significant culinary adventure.

Sarah told Ben about the importance of a nutritional full balance diet. She asked, "Ben, do you know what healthy eating is?"

Ben shrugged his shoulders and said, "Eating food everyday."

Everyone laughed at his innocence.

Then Sarah began to explain, saying, "A balanced diet is the one which involves a range of foods. It is important to ensure that children receive all the nutrients they need for proper growth and development. A proper diet also takes care of overall health. Childrens' healthy diet must to include:

Fruits and vegetables have a major role in a child's nutrition. These foods provide important minerals, vitamins, and fiber. For a wide range of nutrients, go for a colorful variety.

Whole grain bread, brown rice, and oats are among the foods in another category. They are high in fiber and vital nutrients. They promote long-term energy and intestinal health.

For the growth and repair, one should consume proteins. They come from different sources like lean meats, fish, eggs, dairy products, beans, lentils, and nuts.

Eating foods high in calcium is essential for maintaining good bone health. Dairy products contain a lot of calcium. Milk, cheese, and yogurt are examples of dairy products that should be consumed unless there are dietary limitations.

Ethan immediately jumped up and said, "Mom, what do you mean by dietary restrictions?"

"Ethan, some people have lactose tolerance; they can't be driven by dairy products. In such cases, fortified alternatives should be considered." Mr Chatterjee replied.

Children got engrossed in understanding the health benefits of different foods.

While Ben silently but firmly raised a question, "Why do we need this greasy thing? It always spoils my hands." Holding the leg piece in his hand, he asked.

Mrs Chatterjee said, "Ben, These are healthy fats. They are essential for brain development and overall health. Healthy fats come from sources like avocados, nuts, seeds, and oily fish. While the consumption of saturated and trans fats should be limited."

When everyone raised questions, how could little Raj be silent? He asked, "Mom, so, like other food, does sugar and salt also have some significance?"

To that, Michael said, "Of course, Raj. The sugar and salt need to be used in limit.
Overindulgence in salt and sugar can result in health problems like hypertension, obesity, and tooth difficulties. Reducing the consumption of processed foods, sugar-filled beverages, and snacks is crucial.

Michael continued, saying, "Additionally, hydration is crucial. Encouraging water over sugary beverages ensures children stay hydrated without the extra calories and sugar."

Mr Chatterjee nodded in agreement and said, "In my opinion, education about food and nutrition should be age appropriate. Schools should often conduct lectures to help children understand the benefits of various foods. This will enable them to make healthy choices independently."

Everyone seated around the table nodded in agreement with Mr Chatterjee.

Anika, who was silently listening to the talk, raised questions out of her curiosity. She asked, "Why do different areas have such different food habits and traditions? When it comes to different types of food from various cultures, are there sometimes biases? Can we do something to make sure everyone's food traditions are included and respected?"

"Biases in healthy eating may arise from cultural, socioeconomic status, and geographical disparities which impact food choices and views about what defines a healthy diet," Sarah said, placing her hand on her head. It's critical to address these prejudices with compassion and awareness, keeping in mind that different situations call for varied interpretations of healthy eating.

Arpita shared her insight. She said, "Each culture has its unique dietary practices that are often deeply rooted in tradition. Healthy eating initiatives should respect these practices and seek to incorporate traditional foods rather than dismiss them. For example, promoting the nutritional benefits of traditional foods like lentils in Indian diets or fermented vegetables in Korean diets can make healthy eating more relatable and acceptable.

A person's socioeconomic level can frequently restrict their access to healthy foods. In certain places, healthy meals and fresh produce might be costly and difficult to obtain. These obstacles can be lessened with the assistance of laws and initiatives that promote community gardens, subsidize the purchase of healthy foods, and facilitate access to farmers' markets."

"Absolutely right," Michael agreed. "And your dad just mentioned how school can effectively teach this to children."
"Nutrition education ought to be inclusive and flexible to various contexts," he went on. Instead of recommending a one-size-fits-all strategy, it should include information on the fundamentals of balanced eating and how to incorporate them into various dietary plans. This involves engaging community leaders and local nutrition experts who understand the unique needs and preferences of their communities."

"And look at how we've organized this potluck; it demonstrates how the community can instil this in children," said Sarah. She further added, "Encouraging community involvement in creating and implementing healthy eating programs ensures that the initiatives are culturally relevant and supported by the community. This can include cooking classes, community meals, and school programs that celebrate and integrate local culinary traditions with nutritional education."

"Apart from this, we can address the misinformation about what constitutes healthy eating. Public health campaigns should focus on providing clear, evidence-based information that dispels myths and educates people about the importance of a balanced diet." Said Mr Chatterjee.

Sarah further added, "We may develop more inclusive, successful tactics for encouraging a healthy lifestyle that respects and takes into account a variety of ethnic and socioeconomic backgrounds if we acknowledge and overcome these prejudices."

After the lively discussion on food, the kids ran up to Ethan's room for some fun. Moments later, Ethan emerged with a packet of cookies, and Ben came running with a stash of chocolates.

"Children, you just had dinner," Sarah said firmly. "Don't overeat, and remember, eating sweets at night can cause tooth decay."

Ethan frowned. "We've had chocolates plenty of times before. Why are you stopping us now?"

Sarah sighed, crouching to their level. "I know sweets are fun, but eating them right before bed is different. They can stick to your teeth all night and cause cavities. I want you both to have healthy teeth and good sleep."

Ethan grumbled but reluctantly put the cookies back, understanding her point.

The elders met in the living room to continue their conversation on leading by example and promoting healthy eating habits while the children retreated to their rooms. Mr Chatterjee stressed the importance of including children in meal preparation. He said it can be turned into an enjoyable and instructive activity. Arpita recommended adding a variety of vibrant fruits and vegetables to the meals to make them both visually pleasing and nourishing. Michael highlighted the need for regular family meals at the dining table, fostering a routine of balanced eating. Sarah agreed, adding that limiting junk food at home and rewarding healthy choices can also motivate the kids to develop better eating habits.

The parents promised each other that they would adopt and maintain good, healthy eating habits and work to instil these values in their kids.

A family's culture and celebrations revolve around food, which provides a material link to history and customs. The Christmas potluck hosted by the Petersons served as evidence of the power of food to unite people from all backgrounds and promote understanding.

For the Petersons, food served as a means of communication as well as nourishment and affection. Their Christmas traditions revolved around Sarah's roasted turkey and baked cookies, which embodied the coziness and coziness of family get-togethers. These delicacies demonstrated the important part food played in their joyous customs because they were lovingly prepared and shared.

Similarly, the Chatterjee family's biryani, with its flavorful and aromatic spices, represented their Indian ancestry more than merely a dish. Each spice spoke a tale about their native country, and every bite conveyed the history of generations. By sharing their culture with their neighbours over the biryani at the potluck, they promoted mutual respect and a sense of community.

In everyday life, the balance of foods should be carefully maintained. Certain foods are reserved for special occasions. They add to their significance and make celebrations more meaningful. These dishes are enjoyed in moderation, their rarity enhancing their value and the joy they bring.

On the other hand, foods, such as the lentils and vegetables provide essential nutrients and form the backbone of the diets. These foods are prepared regularly, offering consistency and stability in their daily lives. They ensure that the family maintains a balanced diet, rich in the nutrients needed for health and well-being.

The potluck was not just a celebration of food but a celebration of culture and heritage. Each dish was a reflection of the family's identity, a way to honor their roots and share their stories. It was a reminder of the importance of balance in life – that while special foods and celebrations add richness and joy, everyday meals provide the foundation for a healthy and fulfilling life.

The various shapes that food takes have a significant impact on the customs and culture of a household. It serves as a food supply, a vehicle for expression, and a link between the old and the new. Families make memories, transmit cultural traditions, and foster a sense of community via food. A lovely example of this was the potluck hosted by the Petersons, where people from all culinary backgrounds gathered to celebrate the richness and unity of their common human experience.

Creating a pleasant dining atmosphere is another aspect of healthy eating. Promoting consistent mealtimes, family eating dinner together, and mindful eating techniques aids in the development of a positive relationship between kids and food. Since kids often imitate adults, it's critical to provide a positive example for eating habits.

Following up entails staying in touch with communities, evaluating the success of the initiatives, and modifying the course of action in response to input. Ensuring that every child has the chance to form good eating habits also entails supporting local policies that improve food security and education.

Chapter 3- The Unexpected Routine Change

The doorbell rang while the Peterson household was busy getting ready for the holidays. Emma, Sarah's niece, was standing there as Sarah opened the door. Her facial expression was tight and weary. Sarah immediately sensed that something was wrong. She welcomed Emma inside and offered her a seat in the cozy living room.

"Emma, so good to see you! But you look exhausted. What's going on?" Sarah asked with genuine concern.

Emma sighed heavily, sinking into the soft armchair. "Aunt Sarah, it's been really tough lately. Work is overwhelming. Mark and I have been arguing constantly. We don't really have time for one another. I feel as though tension is engulfing me. I came here looking for some quiet time and possibly some guidance."

Michael was decorating the Christmas tree. He joined the conversation, his brow furrowed with worry. "Don't work, Emma. We are there for you. Tell us more about what's been happening."

Emma took a deep breath and began to explain. "It's just... There's no set routine in our lives anymore. Work is demanding. I don't have fix timings. I never know what time I will reach home. Some nights, I don't even eat a proper meal or even get enough sleep. Both my physical and mental health is suffering. Mark feels neglected. I'm so tired, Aunt Sarah. I just want a break from it all."

With her heart pounding for her niece, Sarah listened carefully. "Emma, it sounds like you seem to be under a lot of stress. Establish a routine. It can have a significant impact. In times when life seems chaotic, it can assist to provide some stability and balance."

Emma nodded while tears down her eyes. "But how do I even start? Everything feels so out of control."

Sarah gently placed her hand on Emma's. "You need to start with one step at a time. Take small steps. Set a regular bedtime and wake-up time. Not only for the weekdays, but even on weekends. Try to eat meals at consistent times, and include Mark in these routines. It's important to find time to connect with each other. Even if it is to have a quick breakfast together or a walk in the evening."

Michael went on, "And remember to set aside time for yourself. You need time to relax and engage in activities you enjoy. It's essential for your wellbeing; it's not selfish."

Emma wiped her tears, taking in their advice. "I believe you are correct. We have neglected to care for one another and ourselves because we have been so preoccupied with our busy routines. Maybe if I start setting some routines, things will get better."

Sarah smiled warmly. "Absolutely. Everything won't be solved overnight. But it's ok to have a good start. And always keep this in your mind, it's okay to ask for help. You and Mark need to work as a team. You need to support each other through this."

Emma nodded, feeling hopeful. "I thank both of you. I think I'll take your advice and try to set some routines. And maybe... just maybe, things will start to improve."

Sarah hugged her niece tightly. "You're strong, Emma. You'll get through this. And we're always here for you, no matter what."

Michael smiled reassuringly. "You've got this, Emma. Just take it one day at a time."

Sarah smiled warmly. "Absolutely. It won't solve everything overnight, but it's a good start. And remember, it's okay to ask for help. You and Mark are a team, and you need to support each other through this."

Emma nodded, feeling a glimmer of hope. "Thank you, both of you. I think I'll take your advice and try to establish some routines. And maybe... just maybe, things will start to improve."

Emma groaned once more and remarked, "Aunt Sarah, your guidance is incredible, but there's another issue," just as she was beginning to feel reassured. Even though Emily is only three months old, caring for her and everything else is incredibly demanding.

Sarah's expression softened further. "Emma, raising a child requires full-time labor on your part. I am aware of how difficult it may be, particularly when a baby is so young. However, we also need to discuss something else that is crucial to your future."

Emma looked at her aunt, curious and attentive.

Sarah continued, "I had told you to be careful about having unprotected sex. If you're not careful, you can conceive. Family planning is very important, Emma. This means not having unprotected sex unless you can take responsibility for the consequences. Getting pregnant should be a planned thing, not an accident."

Emma nodded, absorbing her aunt's words.

Before anyone else gets access to your body, you should know how to take care of it and understand your own body," Sarah continued. Knowing what you need and want is important, and you should let your spouse know. This can guarantee that you are both on the same page and help prevent unintended pregnancies."

Emma sighed, ""I suppose we didn't think things through as much as we should have," Emma murmured. I love Emily but all seems so overwhelming."

Sarah nodded. "It's a lot, I know. But now that you're here, let's make a plan. Establishing a routine for Emily can help too. Babies thrive on consistency. Try to set regular feeding and sleeping times for her. This will give you some structure in your day and make it a bit easier to manage your time."

Emma smiled faintly, feeling a bit more hopeful. "Thank you, Aunt Sarah. I'll try to put all this into practice. I am happy that I have your support."

Sarah squeezed her niece's hand. "You're never alone, Emma. We're here for you, always."

Emma felt a newfound feeling of resolve as she headed out that evening. With the help of her family and a strategy to bring some order to her chaotic existence, she felt prepared to take on the difficulties that lay ahead. And she allowed herself to think that things may go better for the first time in a very long time.

Over the next few days, Emma started making small changes. She set a consistent bedtime for Emily and herself, ensuring they both got the rest they needed. She made simple, healthful dinners and set aside specific times for her and Mark to have dinner together. Their hectic lives gradually began to feel more organized as a result of the routines.

Sarah checked in with Emma regularly, offering support and encouragement. One evening when Emma was preparing dinner, she received a call from her aunt.

"Hi, Aunt Sarah! I am so happy to tell you that things are slowly getting better," Emma said, her voice was filled with energy.

"I'm so glad to hear that, Emma. How are you managing everything?" Sarah asked.

"Well, it's not perfect, but having a routine has really helped. Emily's sleep quality has improved. Mark and I have more time to interact. Emma answered, "Although we're still working through our problems, at least we're talking."

"That's wonderful to hear. Remember, it's all about progress, not perfection. Just keep taking it one day at a time," Sarah advised.

Emma sighed with relief. "Thank you, Aunt Sarah. Your advice really made a difference."

Sarah, in the meantime, was thinking back on her own life and the habits she had set up for her family. She came to see how crucial it was to set an example for her own kids as well as Emma. She made the choice to include more family-oriented events that encouraged wholesome routines and solid relationships.

The Petersons' had developed new routines that brought a sense of balance and joy to their lives. Emma noticed the change when she visited them next time. "Wow, Aunt Sarah, you guys seem so happy and energetic. What's your secret?" she asked.

Sarah smiled, "We decided to make some changes too. We established routines. Now we spend quality time together and that has made a big difference. It's not always easy, but it's worth it."

Emma nodded thoughtfully. "I can see that. I'll keep working on our routines and try to incorporate more family activities. Maybe that's what we need too."

As the days passed, Emma and Mark found their groove. The routines brought stability, and their relationship began to heal. They started planning fun activities for weekends, like visiting the park or having picnics. They even planned a small getaway to recharge and reconnect.

****"

Sarah continued to support Emma. She was proud of the progress Emma was making. She knew that with a strong foundation of routines and the love and support of family life challenges can be faced.

One evening, when the kids went to bed Sarah and Michael sitting together thought about how things had changed. "I'm really proud of Emma. She has really worked hard and has come a long way," Sarah said while she was resting her head on Michael's shoulder.

Michael agreed. "She has. And I think we've grown a lot too. Focusing on our routines and spending time together has made us stronger as a family."

Sarah smiled, feeling a deep sense of contentment. "You're correct. The difference is primarily due to the minor things. I'm thankful to our family and our mutual love.

Sitting there in the comfort of their own house, they realized they were prepared to face whatever lay ahead of them. They were committed to continuing to build on the routines they had created, one day at a time, since they were more than just habits—they were the cornerstone of a happy, healthy life.

Emma sat down with Sarah in the cozy living room, watching the serene domestic scene unfold. The Peterson family always appeared to be a well-oiled machine. That runs efficiently despite their hectic schedules. Emma wondered how her aunt pulled it all together with such ease.

"Aunt Sarah, everything looks so perfect here," Emma said, her voice tinged with admiration and a hint of envy. "You and Uncle Michael both have demanding jobs, and yet you seem to have it all together. How do you manage it? It seems so easy for you."

Sarah smiled gently, understanding the weight behind Emma's words. "Emma, believe whatever it might appear from outside, it's not always that way. Trust me it's not that easy. It requires a great deal of work, preparation, and dedication. Allow me to impart some wisdom that has enabled Michael and me to successfully manage our work and personal lives."

She took a moment to gather her thoughts. "First and foremost, it is important for a couple to plan and reconsider their decision to have children.This they should do if they are ambitious and want to take up full fledged careers. Being a parent comes with a lot of responsibility, thus it should not be taken lightly. You must be financially, emotionally, and psychologically prepared for it."

Emma nodded, absorbing every word. "But how do you know whether you're ready for it or not?"

"Well," Sarah continued, "you need to have proper communication and mutual acceptance.It is essential that both partners have a mutual understanding of their roles, expectations, and goals. This clarity will aid in preventing miscommunications and disputes. It's essential to discuss and agree on how you'll manage your time for the child and the career. It is equally important to share responsibilities and support each other."

"Acceptance is key, Emma," Sarah added. "You need to accept that once you are parents, things will change. There will be a shift in your priorities. You will have to make sacrifices. But if you are prepared, then these changes can be beautiful. If you accept them with an open heart, parenthood is a beautiful journey."

Sarah leaned in closer, her tone earnest. "Resources and education are also crucial. Financial stability is important because raising a child is expensive. You should ensure you have a stable income and savings to provide for your child's needs. Additionally, educate yourselves about parenting. Read books, attend workshops, and seek advice from experienced parents. Knowledge is power, and being well-informed will help you navigate the challenges of parenthood."

Emma looked thoughtful. "That really makes sense, Aunt Sarah. But how to be a role model?"

"Being a suitable role model is another most important aspect," Sarah explained. "Children learn by observing their parents. You need to set a good example for them. It is for everything you do, from how you handle stress to how you treat others. Your behavior, values, and attitudes shape their character and the way the world will look at them."

Sarah took a deep breath as she considered her personal experiences, her eyes softened. "Michael and I put a lot of effort into keeping our professional and personal lives in balance. Even if it means making some compromises at work, we place a high priority on spending time with the children.

Emma sighed, feeling a mix of hope and apprehension. "It's a lot to do."

"It is," Sarah agreed. "But remember, if you do not take up small responsibilities together. It will become a difficult journey. It's okay to go slow.. Rushing into parenthood without proper preparation can lead to stress and strain on your relationship and family life."

Emma smiled, feeling a bit more at ease. "Thank you, Aunt Sarah. Your advice is really helpful. I'll take it to heart."

Sarah hugged her niece, her voice filled with warmth and reassurance. "You're welcome, Emma. Just take your time. There's no need to rush. Being a parent is an amazing journey, but it also comes with a lot of responsibility. You'll be an excellent mother, so don't worry."

Emma found Sarah's advice deeply intriguing and insightful. Her curiosity piqued, she asked, "Aunt Sarah, can you tell me more about family, motherhood, and how to raise kids? You make it sound so... manageable."

Sarah smiled, appreciating Emma's eagerness to learn. "Of course, Emma. Creating routines is a crucial part of being a mother and parenting kids. A child's development and sense of security are greatly aided by routines."

Emma leaned in, eager to absorb every bit of wisdom. "Routines?"

"Yes," Sarah nodded. "Creating inner security and routines for a new human being on earth is crucial. A child that follows a consistent schedule knows what to anticipate and when. They feel stable and confident in their surroundings because of this predictability."

Sarah continued, "It's important to give the child the opportunity to influence their own development through understanding. For example, explaining why it's bedtime at a certain hour or why certain foods are healthy helps them comprehend the world around them. This understanding leads to a sense of control and self-awareness."

Emma nodded, seeing the logic in Sarah's words. "So, it's about making them feel secure and understood?"

"Exactly," Sarah said. "The child will adjust if you remain steady and self-assured in your choices. Children feel more secure in the home when they witness their parents being firm and consistent.This internal security is crucial and should not depend on external factors."

She took a time to process what she had said before moving on. Making the child as independent as possible is also crucial. Motivate them to take initiative, make little choices, and grow from their mistakes. Over time, this independence turns into a type of security for the child and the parents."

Emma looked thoughtful. "So, it's about balancing guidance and independence?"

"Yes," Sarah agreed. "You give them the tools to manage the world and prepare them for it at the same time. The goal is to establish a secure atmosphere in which kids can develop, learn, and ultimately flourish independently."

Sarah leaned back, reflecting on her own experiences. "Being a parent is about helping your child make wise decisions and develop self-confidence, not about running their entire life. It's about supporting them, giving them a solid base, then progressively releasing control so they may stand alone."

Emma sighed, feeling both inspired and a little overwhelmed. "It sounds like a lot of responsibility."

It is, Sarah conceded, but it's also quite fulfilling. Among the most wonderful things about being a parent is witnessing your child develop into a self-assured, self-reliant person. And never forget that you are not traveling alone. To assist you on your journey, you have resources, friends, and family."

Emma, inspired by Sarah's wisdom, couldn't help but ask, "Your advice is amazing, Aunt Sarah. But how can a career-oriented couple manage this better and cope with what's about to come?"

Sarah smiled, appreciating Emma's willingness to delve deeper. "Emma, you're right, balancing a profession and raising a family is difficult, but it is absolutely definitely possible with careful planning and a strong relationship. Here are some ideas on how to deal with it more effectively and face the future."

She stopped to gather her thoughts. "The most important thing is to communicate. It is imperative that you and your spouse have honest conversations regarding your expectations, duties, and aspirations. This guarantees that you can effectively support one another and are in agreement."

Emma nodded, understanding the importance of teamwork. Sarah continued, "Next, prioritize your time. It is essential to know what matters the most to you on a personal and professional level. To ensure that you can devote adequate time to your family, you may need to make certain sacrifices or changes to your work options."

"Creating a solid support system is also crucial," Sarah added. "This could include hiring a reliable nanny, leaning on family members, or even forming a network with other parents who can help out when needed. Having dependable support can significantly ease the pressure and give you peace of mind."

Sarah's tone became more empathetic as she said, "Flexibility is another important aspect. Be prepared to adjust and modify as necessary. It's acceptable for things to not always go according to plan. Being adaptable makes it easier to deal with unforeseen difficulties."

Emma listened intently, appreciating the practical advice. "Making time for your family is also very important, Sarah underlined. Making sure that the time you do spend with your child is meaningful and fulfilling is more important than necessarily spending every waking second with them. As we previously discussed, routines can assist in providing your children with a secure environment."

Sarah leaned in closer, her voice filled with warmth. "It's critical that you look after your needs. Taking care of your physical, emotional, and mental well-being is essential if you want to maintain the stamina and patience needed for both job and raising a child. This can include setting aside time for pastimes, exercise, or simply relaxing.

Emma sighed, feeling a bit overwhelmed but also inspired. "It sounds like a lot, Aunt Sarah. How do you manage to juggle everything?"

Sarah chuckled softly. "At first, it could feel overwhelming, but remember that the objective is development, not perfection. Michael and I try to keep our cool and support one another in spite of the challenges we have endured together."

Finally, she said, "Never undervalue the significance of living in the now. Try to give it your all whether you're with your family or at work. This mindfulness can help you manage stress better and appreciate the small joys of both your professional and personal life."

Emma listened attentively to Sarah's wisdom, absorbing every bit of advice. But she still felt the weight of her responsibilities and sought further guidance. "Aunt Sarah," she began hesitantly, "how do you manage to take on so much responsibility and guide your children so effectively? It feels overwhelming."

Sarah gave Emma a reassuring smile. "Emma, it's natural to feel overwhelmed, especially at the beginning. But remember, you've chosen to take on this incredible responsibility of guiding a new person on this earth. Your child arrives with its own karma and purpose. The sooner you understand your own role and your child's task in life, the easier it will be for the child to understand their direction and why they chose you as their role model on this planet."

Emma looked intrigued, yet puzzled. "How do I even begin to understand that, Aunt Sarah?"

Sarah leaned in closer, her voice soft but firm. "It starts with understanding and accepting your own journey and purpose. It is simpler to teach your child your beliefs and aspirations when you are clear about them yourself. By your deeds, demonstrate to them what it is to lead a meaningful and worthwhile life. Don't be afraid to make lifestyle or employment adjustments to ensure security and stability.Children thrive in stable environments where they feel secure."

Emma nodded, her eyes showing a mix of understanding and uncertainty. "But what if I don't always know what my purpose is or how to guide them properly?"

Sarah extended her hand to grab Emma's. "It's acceptable to not know everything at once. Being a parent is a process of mutual learning and development. Have patience with both your child and yourself. Trust that you will find your way, and so will they. Children have incredibly strong, developing minds. They often take responsibility for their own development in ways we might not even realize."

Emma seemed more at ease but still had questions. "How do I balance guiding them without imposing too much?"

Sarah smiled warmly. "Let them follow their hobbies and support their freedom. Give them direction and encouragement, but give them the latitude to choose for themselves and gain experience from their mistakes. This balance will help them develop confidence and resilience."

Emma took a deep breath, feeling more grounded. "Thank you, Aunt Sarah. Your advice always makes things seem more manageable."

Sarah squeezed Emma's hand gently. "Remember, Emma, being a parent is about being a guide and a role model. Be patient, loving, and understanding with your child. Give them a secure environment so they can develop and flourish. Above all, have faith in your own abilities to produce a great, capable human being."

Emma smiled, feeling a renewed sense of hope and determination. "I will, Aunt Sarah. Thank you for always being there for me. Your advice means a lot to me. I'll try to incorporate routines and stability into our lives and help Emily grow into a strong, independent person."

Sarah hugged Emma, filled with pride and love. "You're welcome, dear. You'll be a fantastic mommy. Just keep in mind that you are not traveling alone. I'm here to support you at every step of the road. You may have a good profession and a happy family life at the same time provided you have the correct attitude and support system. And whenever you need assistance, I'll be here to provide it."

With the promise of a better future for the coming generation and their common wisdom, their friendship became stronger as they sat together. Emma felt more prepared to take on the responsibilities of parenting.She knew she had some important decisions to make. she also felt more equipped to make them, knowing she had a strong support system and valuable guidance from her beloved aunt.

Chapter 4 - The Interfaith Friendship

The Chatterjees and the Petersons were next door neighbors. Over the years, despite coming from different cultural and religious origins, they had forged a close friendship. The Petersons are Christians, while the Chatterjees followed Hinduism. They frequently got together for dinners, celebrated one other's holidays, and helped each other through the highs and lows of life.

At a community function, the two families had initially been acquainted. They discovered that, despite their differences, they had similar values—like respect, compassion, and the value of family—after getting to know one another. They frequently went to one other's family get-togethers or played together in the local park. This bond across cultures gave both families a special chance to understand and respect each other's customs and beliefs.

Ethan and Ben, the Petersons' kids, were playing in the front yard one Sunday morning. Just then, Mrs. Chatterjee greeted Sarah Peterson with a warm smile. They started a conversation. Mrs. Chatterjee invited the Petersons to Anika's birthday party, which they were planning to celebrate with a few close friends in the evening.

Sarah accepted the invitation with a smile. The party was arranged in the backyard. Everyone enjoyed the cool breeze and the chirping of birds. Arpita noticed an unusual expression on Ethan's face, as if something was bothering him.

"What is the matter, Ethan?" Arpita asked with a warm smile.

Ethan took a deep breath, and glanced down at his feet. "Well, on Monday, we have an essay writing competition at school. It is about religion and beliefs. Honestly speaking I have no clue what to write."

Arpita's eyes shined with understanding. "Oh, that sounds challenging. But at the same time, it is also a great opportunity to learn. What's bothering you about it?"

With a shrug, Ethan lowered his shoulders. "I simply have no idea where to begin. There are so many religions around the world. Individuals hold unique beliefs. I'm not sure how to write about them all."

Arpita thought for a moment before replying; then she leaned forward, her voice gentle and encouraging."Start with what you know, Ethan. Talk about your own beliefs and traditions, and then explore how different families, like ours, have their own unique practices. You can write about how understanding and respecting each other's beliefs can bring people closer, just like our families have become friends despite our different backgrounds."

Ethan's face brightened a little. "That makes sense. I can write about how celebrating Diwali with you guys was so much fun and how you came over for Christmas with us. It's like we learn from each other."

"Exactly," Arpita said, giving him a reassuring pat on the back. "Focus on the common values we share and how our different beliefs make our friendships richer. I'm sure you'll write a wonderful essay."

Ethan smiled, feeling more confident and grateful for Arpita's advice. He couldn't wait to start his essay and share his thoughts about the beauty of diversity and mutual respect.

"Hey, Arpita, I am so grateful to you. You have handled him well. He often asks me,
why do the Chatterjees celebrate Diwali? How do you discuss different religions and ideas with your kids, Arpita?" Sarah asked, genuinely curious.

""Talking about different religions and ideas with children can be challenging. But it's crucial to create an atmosphere of respect and understanding between people. " Arpita said.

Sarah smiled, I am so happy that now I have an opportunity to discuss such important topics. Sarah said, "Ethan, you had asked about the Diwali festival the other day. Listen carefully, Diwali is a Hindu festival that honors the victory of good over evil and light over darkness," Sarah explained. There are loads of lights, sweets, and family get-togethers throughout this lovely event."

Ethan asked, "Why do they light lamps during Diwali?"

Arpita smiled, " Lighting lamps symbolizes this and brings positivity into our homes."

In return, Raj asked, "Why do you celebrate Christmas?"

Michael explained,"Christmas is a celebration of Jesus Christ's birth," Michael clarified. It's a season of happiness, generosity, and spending time with those you care about. We spread happiness by exchanging gifts and decking our homes with lights.It's time to reflect on the love and teachings of Jesus."

Mr. and Mrs. Chatterjee joined the discussion to give their viewpoints. Mr. Chatterjee praised the fact that the questions were posed. "Understanding the other religions enables us to respect the diversity in our world."

"It's essential to acknowledge and respect each other's beliefs," Arpita continued. We hope you will respect our traditions as much as we respect yours."

Sarah nodded in agreement. "Absolutely. Realizing that every individual has the right to hold any opinion they choose is essential. The Chatterjees chose to practice Hinduism, just as we do Christianity. Both are personal and individual choices that deserve respect."

Michael added thoughtfully, "We believe in teaching our kids that our faith is a personal journey. It's something we've chosen for ourselves and we appreciate others because they have the same freedom to follow their own path. This contributes to the atmosphere that fosters respect and safety for all people."

Arpita went on to say, "We ensure that everyone in our family has the opportunity to express their ideas. This means asking questions, listening, and occasionally participating in one another's customs. It's about fostering a sense of security and understanding within the family."

Mr. Chatterjee nodded, "That's right. For instance, during Diwali, we invite the Petersons over to join our celebrations. They get to experience our traditions firsthand, which helps build mutual respect and understanding."

Sarah added, "And we do the same for Christmas. Inviting the Chatterjees over for our Christmas dinner allows them to see how we celebrate and what it means to us. This exchange of traditions enriches our lives and broadens our perspectives."

With a nod, Sarah said, "I've been thinking how to respectfully and meaningfully convey to Ethan and Ben about varied customs. Let's discuss this over some tea. Maybe we can come up with a plan together."

Sarah explained to the children that their beliefs are personal choices. "You have the freedom to believe in what feels right to you," she said. "But remember, everyone else has that same freedom. It's important to respect the choices they make, just as you would want them to respect your choices."

Arpita too shared her sentiments. She said "Our beliefs are our own, and they guide us in our lives," she told them. "But it's equally important to understand that others may have different beliefs that are just as important to them."

Sarah and Arpita both decided to create an open environment where their children could ask questions and express their thoughts freely. Sarah and Michael, along with Arpita and Mr. Chatterjee made it a point to sit down with their kids regularly to discuss various topics, including religion.

One evening, as they gathered in Chatterjee's living room, the children were encouraged to share what they knew about each other's religions.

The Petersons and Chatterjees decided to participate in each other's celebrations to give their children a practical understanding of different religions. This hands-on approach allowed the kids to experience the richness of each tradition.

During Janmashtami, the Petersons helped the Chatterjees decorate their home with flowers. Ethan and Ben enjoyed the sweets and the other preparations. They learnt about the significance of each ritual. It was similarly the way the Chatterjee family had joined the Petersons in decorating the Christmas tree, singing carols, and exchanging gifts during Christmas.

The next day of Janmashtami, Ethan was curious to know about the festival. "Ethan, it's okay to be curious about other people's beliefs. However, you should ask questions with respect so that they don't hurt the sentiments. Secondly, listen to their answers with an open mind." Sarah told Ethan. "

Sarah further explained, "Understanding doesn't mean you have to change your beliefs. It means you acknowledge and respect someone else's beliefs. Acceptance is about recognizing that our differences make us unique and that's something to celebrate."

Michael looked at the kids playing together and smiled. "Seeing our children play and grow together is the best part. They learn from each other and develop an innate respect for different cultures and beliefs. It's a powerful lesson that will stay with them for life."

The parents talked about handling disagreements and possible problems that could result from their differing worldviews as they went along.

"Sometimes, our beliefs might clash," Michael acknowledged. "However it's important to handle the differences carefully. We should not see them as barriers, but as opportunities to learn and grow."

"Exactly," Mr. Chatterjee agreed. Rather than passing judgment when we see differences, we should approach them with curiosity. Potential disputes can be transformed into worthwhile learning opportunities by asking questions. We can try to understand, and remain ready to value new information."

Arpita shared a recent event, saying, "Anika was hesitant to participate in several activities when she was invited to a school Christmas party. After discussing, we came to the conclusion that it is acceptable to participate in the celebration while upholding our personal beliefs. Finding a balance and honoring other people's customs as well as our own is important."

Sarah nodded, "We've had similar discussions with Ethan and Ben. We encourage them to participate in their friends' cultural and religious activities, while also staying grounded in our own beliefs. It's about mutual respect and understanding."

Michael stressed how crucial it is to instill in kids a sense of personal accountability for their beliefs. " As parents, it is our responsibility to guide our children. We need to instill in them the idea that their beliefs are their own and that they must take responsibility for them."

Sarah added, "Being stable and confident in our decisions helps our children feel secure. We are their role models. When they see us respecting our own beliefs and that of others, they learn to do the same. It's crucial for creating a harmonious and inclusive environment."

Arpita shared, "We also make it a point to discuss why we follow certain practices and what they mean to us. This helps our children understand the deeper significance of our traditions and respect them."

As the sun began to set, the parents felt a renewed sense of commitment to create an environment of respect and understanding.

"We're all together in this," Mr. Chatterjee said, looking at his friends. "We will support each other and teach our children these values. Thus, we can create a community that will celebrate diversity and unity."

Sarah smiled, "And that's the beauty of our friendship. Even though we are from different backgrounds, we support each other. We are learning from each other's traditions and customs. It's a wonderful example for our children."

Michael concluded, "Let's continue to build this foundation of respect and understanding. By doing so, we are enriching our own lives and at the same time teaching our children the importance of accepting diversity."

Arpita added, "At times it may seem difficult for us to always understand each other's practices. However we can always respect them. It's about teaching our children to appreciate the differences and see the value in other cultures."

Michael nodded in agreement. "Exactly. Forcing children to adhere strictly to religious practices can often backfire. Instead, by letting them witness and participate voluntarily, we nurture their curiosity and respect. They're more likely to embrace these traditions if they feel connected to them on their own terms."

Sarah chimed in, "It's also crucial to let them ask questions and express their doubts. Open dialogue helps them form a deeper, more personal connection with their beliefs. We should be their guides, not their dictators."

Mr. Chatterjee said, "I remember my own childhood days. My parents gave me freedom. They never imposed anything on me. They practiced their faith sincerely, and I naturally followed suit because I saw the peace and joy it brought them. I want the same for my children."

Ethan, overhearing the adults, asked, "So, you're saying it's okay if I don't follow everything exactly like you do?"

Arpita smiled warmly at him. "Yes, Ethan. It's about understanding and finding your own way.All we want is for you to grow up appreciating and respecting all beliefs, including your own.

The discussion brought to light the common beliefs of the Chatterjees and the Petersons, namely that the goal of religious education should be to create an atmosphere in which kids feel free to investigate, challenge, and eventually accept their own spirituality rather than to submit to strict rules.

As the evening continued, the children played together, embodying the harmony and understanding their parents spoke of. The ideals that were being taught—values that went beyond religious boundaries and included acceptance, love, and respect—were best demonstrated by their laughing and companionship. "The ultimate objective is to develop compassionate, open-minded individuals,"

Michael stated in his conclusion. They pick up this trait when they witness us respecting one another's beliefs. They will benefit greatly from this present for the rest of their lives.

Sarah added, "And remember, our actions speak louder than words. By living our values and showing respect, we set a powerful example for our kids."

As the children played happily in the backyard and the men went inside to have drinks, Sarah and Arpita found themselves alone on the patio, the warm evening air filled with the sounds of laughter and distant cricket chirps. Sarah leaned back in her chair, a thoughtful look crossing her face.

"Arpita, can I ask you something?" she began, her tone gentle.

"Of course, Sarah. What's on your mind?" Arpita replied, turning to face her friend.

"I've always admired you and Mr. Chatterjee for the way you both manage your household. You both have a strong Hindu background, yet I've seen that both of you have different beliefs. How do you manage that? Especially when it comes to children?" Sarah asked with genuine curiosity. There was concern in her voice.

Arpita smiled softly. She took a moment to gather her thoughts. "Certainly, it's not always easy, Sarah.Mr Chatterjee and I do have different approaches to our faith. He's more traditional. However, I've always believed in a more flexible spirituality. My religion is the belief in myself and my abilities. I've created my own limits according to my own ability. I constantly evaluate and re-evaluate my beliefs. I'm not bound by any one religion. I use traditions from several different religions that I think best fits in that moment and the place."

Sarah nodded, intrigued. "That sounds... liberating. Does it ever cause conflict between you two?"

Arpita took a deep breath and held a smile on her lips. "Sometimes. Mr. Chatterjee's values the rituals and the structure they bring. He finds comfort in the traditions he grew up with. I deeply respect that. For me, spirituality is more fluid. I draw from various traditions—Hindu, Buddhist, even some Christian practices—whatever feels right at that moment. It's more about the essence than the form for me."

Sarah moved forward, her curiosity rising up. "How do you reconcile that? Especially with the kids? Don't they get confused?"

Arpita shook her head. "Not really. We make it a point to explain our perspectives to Anika and Raj. We tell them that while dad likes to follow certain rituals, while mom believes in a more personal approach. It's important for them to know and understand that there are different ways to connect with the divine. It's okay to find your own path."

There was a hint of concern still in Sarah's eyes. "I am still confused. How do you ensure they don't feel torn between your different beliefs?"

Arpita placed a reassuring hand on Sarah's arm. "By being honest and open to them. We've given them an environment where they can clear their confusion and express their concerns. We encourage them to explore their own paths and find what resonates with them. It's not only about choosing one over the other, it is also about understanding and respecting both."

Sarah slowly but firmly tries to digest Arpita's words. "That makes a lot of sense. I have always been more traditional in my faith. But I value what you're saying. It's about finding a balance, isn't it?"

Arpita agreed. ""Exactly. It's important to remember that spirituality is a personal journey. What works for one person might not work for another. By giving our children the freedom to explore and discover their own beliefs, we're helping them develop a deeper, more personal connection to their faith."

Sarah smiled, feeling a sense of relief. "I appreciate you shared this with me, Arpita. It's given me a lot to think about."

Arpita returned the smile. "Anytime, Sarah. We're all in this together, trying to do the best we can for our families."

The conversation moved onlighter topics. Yet Sarah's mind felt heavy with the discussion they had. She was impressed by Arpita's approach. She wondered how she could apply some of that adaptability into her own family's life.

Later that evening when men returned with their drinks, Sarah noticed the growing friendship between the two families. It was an evidence of their close connection and mutual respect for one another's differences.

"Arpita, have you ever faced any significant challenges because of your differing beliefs?" Sarah asked, steering the conversation back to their earlier discussion.

Arpita thought for a moment before responding. "Yes, there have been times when it was challenging. For example, during festivals. Mr. Chatterjee prefers to follow traditional practices, and I sometimes feel disconnected from them. But we've learned to compromise. I participate in the rituals out of respect for him, and he respects my need for a more personal, introspective approach to spirituality."

Sarah nodded, understanding the complexity of such a dynamic. "It must require a lot of patience and understanding."

"It does," Arpita agreed. "But it's worth it. The key is communication and mutual respect. We've learned to see our differences not as obstacles, but as opportunities to grow and learn from each other."

Sarah felt a deep admiration for her friend. "I hope I can teach Ethan and Ben to be as open-minded and respectful as Anika and Aarav."

"You already are, Sarah," Arpita said warmly. "Just by having this conversation, you're showing a willingness to understand and grow. That's a powerful example for your children."

The two mothers watched their children play and heard the sound of discussion coming from inside the house while they sat in amicable silence for a little while. It was a lovely evening, full of the promise of greater understanding and the warmth of friendship.

As the night drew on, the families gathered together for dinner. Over dessert, Michael raised a toast. "To friendship and understanding. May we always respect and appreciate our uniqueness and appreciate who we are."

The clinking of glasses and the shared smiles around the table was a moment of unity. It was an expression that they were all part of one extended family.

Sarah had a newfound feeling of purpose as the evening drew to an end and the family said their final goodbyes. She was committed to providing a space where her kids could freely explore their faith without worrying about being judged or forced to do anything. She wanted them to understand that faith was a personal journey. They too had the right to choose their own path.

In the following weeks, Sarah and Michael had several conversations with Ethan and Ben about faith and beliefs. They encouraged their children to explore different religions. They explained that while they followed Christianity, there were many other paths to spirituality. It was important to respect them all.

One Sunday afternoon, as the family gathered in the living room, Ethan asked, "Mom, can you tell us more about Hinduism? I'm curious about what Mr. Chatterjee believes."

Sarah smiled. She felt grateful as she had an opportunity to broaden her child's understanding. "Of course, Ethan. Hinduism is one of the oldest religions in the world. It's a rich and diverse tradition.

InHinduism people worship many gods and goddesses. Each of them represents different aspects of life."

Ben, who had been listening quietly, asked, "Like how we have saints?"

"Yes, exactly," Sarah replied. "And just like in Christianity, Hinduism also teaches values like kindness, respect, and the importance of family."

Ethan nodded thoughtfully. "I think it's cool that we have friends who believe in different things. It makes life more interesting."

Michael, who had been reading a book on the couch, looked up and added, "And it teaches us to be open-minded and accepting of others. That's one of the most important lessons we can learn."

One evening, as they were getting ready for bed, Ethan said to his mother, "Mom, I'm glad we have friends like Anika and Raj. They've taught me so much about different cultures and beliefs."

Sarah hugged her son, feeling proud. "I'm glad too, Ethan. Remember that the world is full of different people with different beliefs. The more we understand and respect each other, the better we can make our world."

As she tucked him into bed, Sarah thought about the journey they had been on. It wasn't always easy, but it was worth it. She had been able to develop a sense of respect and understanding in her children. This was one of the most valuable gifts she could give them.

And in that small suburban neighborhood, the seeds of acceptance and understanding were sown, promising a future where differences were celebrated, and the bonds of friendship were unbreakable.

The families of Peterson and Chatterjee served as living examples of the value of respect and understanding between people. They fostered a peaceful home where their kids could develop and learn via open conversation, sharing of experiences, and a dedication to respecting one another's values.

Differences were not viewed as obstacles in this lively neighborhood, but rather as chances to appreciate the distinctive qualities of every faith. The families understood that by creating an atmosphere of respect for each other, they were improving their own lives as well as imparting lifelong values to their offspring.

The bond between the families was strengthened not just by shared experiences, but by the mutual respect and understanding that underpinned their relationship. The Petersons and the Chatterjees had created a microcosm of what they hoped the world could be—a place where diversity is celebrated and differences are embraced with open hearts and minds.

Chapter 5 - The Lost Tradition

Arpita Chatterjee, stood at the kitchen window and looked out. The houses in the street were arranged in orderly rows. There was calmness in the streets and were illuminated by a gentle glow in the early morning light. Arpita's new life was secured and comfortable.Yet she still felt as though something was missing, especially when Rakshabandhan was approaching.

Rakshabandhan is traditionally a time for gathering and joy in India. Sisters would adorn their brother's wrist with a sacred thread known as a rakhi during the festivities.It signifies love and protection. Arpita recalled those lively days filled with laughter when family gathered for the celebrations. She remembered her brother and the colorful rakhis she tied and the gifts she received.

This year, however, the festival felt distant. The expectations and routines of living in a foreign land seemed to be displacing the cultural customs she had grown up with. She let out a heavy sigh and turned away from the window to see Anika and Raj, her kids, still deep in their morning routines.

.

"Anika, Raj, can we talk for a minute?" she called softly.

Sensing the gravity in her tone, the kids glanced up from their games and came to sit with her at the kitchen table.

"What's troubling you, Mom?" Raj asked, his young face filled with concern.

Arpita hesitated for a moment, gathering her thoughts. "Rakshabandhan is coming up soon. One of our unique festivals is this one. It's a time to honor the relationship between siblings. However, things won't be the same this year. I worry that we are going to forget about our traditions."

Anika has always been perceptive. She took her mother's hand. "We can still celebrate it, Mom. Even if we're not in our country, we can still keep our traditions alive."

Arpita smiled and appreciated her daughter's optimism. "I know, sweetheart. It's just that it feels so far away. I miss the way we used to celebrate with all our family around us."

Raj, trying to cheer his mother up, said, "We have each other, right? We can make new traditions here. Maybe we can invite our friends and show them how we celebrate Rakshabandhan."

Arpita felt a surge of pride at her children's resilience. She said to herself developing hope within. "They were right. Even if we are away from India we will surely try to keep our culture alive. It might not be the same. I know, they will find new ways to honor their traditions."

"You're right, Raj. We can create our own celebrations here," she said, feeling a renewed sense of determination. "How about we make some rakhis together and prepare some of the traditional sweets? We can share the significance of the festival with our friends and neighbors."

Anika's eyes lit up with excitement. "That sounds like a great idea, Mom! I can help with the decorations, and Raj can help you make the sweets."

For the next few days, they spent planning and preparing for Rakshabandhan. Along with sharing her childhood stories, Arpita taught her children how to make rakhis. She taught them to put the beads in the thread and tie knots to make rakhis. They cooked traditional dishes. Their entire house was filled with the familiar aromas. This brought back memories of their hometown.

They invited their friends from the neighborhood to celebrate Rakshabandhan with them. The Petersons also joined in the celebration. Arpita explained the significance of the festival to everyone. Anika, then proudly tied rakhi on Raj's wrist. Symbolizing their bond and commitment to protect each other.

The celebration was beautiful. It was a blend of old traditions and new beginnings. Arpita realized that they hadn't lost their culture, as they shared food and laughter with their friends. Instead, they had found a way to adapt it to their new life. This celebration created a bridge between the past and the present.

That evening, Arpita was very happy and was filled with a sense of contentment. She hadn't felt it in a long time.Though they were far from home, yet their cultural traditions were still a part of their lives. She realized the essence of who they were will always remain.

The next day, Sarah came to meet Arpita. "The arrangements and planning were fantastic," she praised. Arpita smiled and said, "It wasn't my plan; it was the children's idea." Sarah felt proud and told Arpita, "You've raised them so well. Your parenting style is truly admirable."

It is the influence of your parenting style. You taught them the important of balancing between individuality and instilling a sense of community. Actually it is true, the core principle revolves around placing the individual at the center. It is about understanding that each person is a part of a larger whole. This is about creating a balance to make sure that children grow up with a strong sense of self-worth and identity. It also helps in understanding their role and responsibilities within their family. To know that they are a part of community, and society as whole.

It also emphasizes individuality.Giving kids the chance to explore their individual personalities, skills, and interests is vital. Children are encouraged to follow their passions, take independent action, and grow from their experiences. For instance, we should provide them the tools if they have an interest in art. We should give them time to pursue this interest. They may have a stronger sense of self and confidence as a result. Children benefit from this individualized approach by feeling appreciated and cherished for who they are.

Arpita nodded in agreement. She said, "Absolutely. I think it's important to strike a balance between encouraging children to be unique and teaching them about their role in society. Kids need to learn that while personal growth is vital, they are also members of a family, a community, and a society. They rely on respect, cooperation, and assistance to one another. Values like empathy, respect for others, and the significance of adding to the group's well-being should be ingrained. Family talks, community service projects, and group projects are examples of activities that foster collaboration and can teach kids the value of cooperating and supporting one another.

Other essential elements of this parenting style include comprehending and elucidating the rationale behind various behaviors as well as the workings of society. It is insufficient to merely instruct kids; they also need to comprehend the thinking behind choices and behaviors. This improves children's understanding of the world and enhance critical thinking in them. For example, children can better understand the bigger picture and the consequences of their actions when the reasoning for rules and boundaries is explained to them.This method not only fosters compliance but also helps kids internalize morals and values, which results in more considerate and accountable behavior.

In addition, parents ought to provide an example for their children in the behavior they value. The kindness, respect, and responsibility that parents demonstrate in their daily lives has a significant impact on children. Parents need to set an example of the values they want their children to follow. As children learn a lot from watching their parents. This means parents need to be open to new ideas. They have to be considerate of the opinions of others. They also have to practice what they preach about being involved in the community and taking personal responsibility.

This parenting style emphasizes a strong environment where children feel they are understood. They feel respected, and safe. It gives them a platform where they are heard. It is about being there in their life, and providing consistent guidance and support. This style encourages children to feel at ease in expressing their thoughts and feelings. It deepens the relationship between parents and children and promotes mutual respect and trust.

A few days later, Sarah invited Arpita over coffee. The aroma of freshly brewed coffee welcomed her. They both made themselves comfortable in the living room. "Everything was just perfect on Rakshabandhan," Sarah said as she made herself comfortable on the armchair. "Everything was magical. The decorations, the food and the entire atmosphere added to the celebration."

Arpita's eyes shined as she felt a sense of pride."Thank you, Sarah. But truly speaking, Anika and Raj should be given the credit. After all it was their idea and effort. " Sarah was Impressed and she said, "You've truly done an incredible job raising them, Arpita. Your parenting is inspirational."

Sarah began, "I've always believed that customs and practices are the heartbeat of family life. They provide a sense of identity and continuity, connecting generations."

Arpita nodded in agreement. "Absolutely. For us, celebrating festivals like Diwali, Holi, and Raksha Bandhan not only keeps us connected to our roots but also imparts valuable lessons to our children. It teaches them about their heritage and the values we hold dear."

Sarah reflected on her own experiences. "I truly agree with what you say. For us also, Christmas and Thanksgiving are not just about the festivities but are about coming together as a family. It is about sharing gratitude, and reinforcing the bonds we share. Michael and I make sure that Ethan and Ben understand the significance behind these celebrations rather than just enjoying and having fun."

The friendship between the Petersons and the Chatterjees exemplified a beautiful blend of traditions. Their children had grown up participating in both sets of customs, gaining a unique perspective and appreciation for diversity.

Arpita shared, "Last Diwali, I saw that Ethan and Ben were equally excited about the preparations as Raj and Anika. They helped in making rangoli and lighting diyas. They even tried their hand at making sweets. It was heartwarming to see them so involved."

Sarah laughed. "And last Christmas, Raj and Anika were the stars of our nativity play. They learned the carols and sang with us. Raj helped Michael and Ethan in decorating the Christmas tree. Anika helped me with the Christmas dinner. It's these shared experiences that broaden their horizons.This teaches them the importance of respect and inclusion."

Customs and practices also acts as a medium to instill values. Arpita explained, "Our festivals teach our children about the victory of good over evil. They learn the value of family as well as the necessity of kindness and giving." the importance of family, and the need for compassion and generosity."

"We go around the table during Thanksgiving and every individual shares what they're grateful for," Sarah continued. Although it's an easy exercise, it teaches the kids to be grateful and to recognize their blessings."

However, it was not easy to maintain these customs as immigrants in a foreign country. Arpita reflected, "When we first arrived here, it was difficult to keep up with all of our traditions. But over time, we found ways to adapt. We might not celebrate every festival with the same grandeur, but we make sure to keep the essence alive."

Sarah nodded. "It's about finding a balance. We too have had to adapt some of our practices to fit our modern lifestyle. The important thing is to ensure that the core values and lessons are passed on."

Both women agreed that these customs had a profound impact on their children. Arpita noted, "Raj and Anika have grown up with a strong sense of identity. They are proud of their heritage and respectful of other cultures."

Sarah smiled. "Ethan and Ben have become more open-minded and empathetic. They understand that different families have different traditions, and they respect that."

Their children's friendship had flourished in this rich tapestry of customs and practices. They had learned to appreciate the beauty in diversity and to find common ground in shared values.

They talked on the value of preserving these customs for the coming generation during their conversation. Arpita responded, "It's our duty to ensure that our kids not only actively indulge in these traditions but also acknowledge their importance."

Sarah agreed. "And it's also important to allow them to create their own traditions. Michael and I always involve Ethan and Ben in the planning of our celebrations. We want them to feel a sense of ownership and pride in these practices."

By weaving together the threads of their cultural heritage and modern life, the Petersons and Chatterjees were building a legacy for their children. A legacy that celebrated diversity, fostered understanding, and upheld the values that formed the bedrock of their families.

Arpita concluded, "Customs and practices are not just about the past. They also create a future where children can live with a strong sense of who they are. It tells them where they come from."

Sarah smiled warmly. "And in doing so, we ensure that the heartbeat of our families continues to resonate through the generations."

Both the women felt grateful for the rich cultural identity that had woven their friendship. They knew that they were nurturing a future where children are developing respect and understanding about different cultures. Their shared values would guide their children, just as customs and practices had guided them.

On a weekend both the families went for a picnic. As Sarah and Arpita sat down to sip coffee, their conversation naturally shifted to parenting. They discussed the unique challenges it brought along. Arpita began, "Do you know raising children in a multicultural environment has its own set of issues. But it's also incredibly enriching." Sarah nodded, understanding the delicate balance required to honor their distinct heritages while fostering a shared identity in their new home.

"How do you manage to explain these cultural differences to your kids?" Sarah asked. Arpita smiled thoughtfully. "I always start emphasizing and explaining that at core we are all human beings. We are united by humanity even though we may come from different cultures and traditions. It's important to explain heritage and environment, and why different characteristics have developed in different races. I often use examples from nature to make it relatable. For instance, animals develop certain traits based on their habitats, and similarly, humans adapt to their environments. This helps them understand why we look and sometimes act differently but also underscores our shared human experience."

Sarah nodded, intrigued by Arpita's approach. "That's a beautiful way to frame it. It's essential for children, especially in blended families or with adopted siblings, to understand and respect these differences."

Sarah continued, " I get your point. We are all human beings on this earth in different forms and take on different colors and shapes. So true, it is important to explain heritage and environment. It is also important that they know why different characteristics have developed in different races."

Arpita said, "To help children understand this, using analogies from the animal kingdom can be very effective. Let me give you examples of polar bears and the camel. A polar bear has thick white fur and a layer of fat to keep it warm in the freezing Arctic environment. This white fur also helps it blend in with the snow. It becomes easier for it to hunt and avoid predators. A camel has a hump to store fat and can go for long periods without water. This helps it survive in the hot, arid deserts. Its long eyelashes and closable nostrils protect it from sandstorms.

Sarah interrupted and said, "So you mean to say that just like these animals, we humans have also adapted to our environments over thousands of years. People from different parts of the world have developed unique physical characteristics. They have different cultural practices that help them to survive in their specific environments. For instance, people with darker skin have more melanin, to protect against the harmful effects of the sun's UV rays. This makes it easier for them to live in sunny, equatorial regions. That's a great way to explain it to children."

"These examples will help children see that these differences are natural adaptations to the environment. It will promote a sense of appreciation and respect for the diversity in human appearances and cultures." Sarah added.

Arpita continued, "Social differences, however, are choices we make. It's important that they know the consequences of the choices they make. It is essential to understand the importance of respecting social rules in different contexts. We need to teach them to navigate through these complexities with empathy and understanding."

The conversation deepened. They explored the nuances of parenting in a multicultural world. They shared insights and strategies to ensure their children grew up with compassion.

As the evening settled into a comfortable rhythm, the children returned from their play, their faces flushed with excitement. Sarah and Arpita watched them fondly, their conversation transitioning seamlessly to the topic of managing and discussing cultural differences with children.

Arpita began, "We have made it a point to celebrate both Hindu and Christian festivals. We tell stories about various festivals and explain their significance. We tell them the values they represent."

Sarah added, "We do something similar. We want our children to see that these celebrations are more than just traditions. They help us to connect with our roots and with each other. It's a beautiful way to learn and celebrate togetherness."

Arpita nodded. "Exactly. We make it relatable by using tales and analogies, and it's important to be upfront about the unique backgrounds of adopted children and mixed families.For instance, we might compare cultural traits to how different animals adapt to their environments. Our cultural characteristics enable us to maintain a connection to our past, just as a polar bear's thick fur aids in its survival in the cold."

"That's a great analogy," Sarah said, impressed. "It makes the concept so accessible for kids."

Arpita smiled. "Yes, and it fosters a sense of pride in their own identity while also cultivating respect for others. We also emphasize that social differences are choices. We explain the social rules and their consequences. It helps them to understand why certain behaviors are acceptable in some contexts but not in others. This teaches them to be empathetic and adaptable."

Sarah agreed, "That's so important. We've also had conversations about the impact of our choices on others. It's about building a moral compass based on empathy and respect."

As the evening wore on, the conversation delved deeper into practical strategies for managing these discussions.

Arpita shared, "One thing we do is family storytelling nights. Each family member gets to share a story from their heritage. It's a fun way to learn and appreciate our diverse backgrounds."

Sarah nodded, "We do something similar. And we encourage our kids to ask questions. No question is too silly. It's about creating an open dialogue."

Arpita added, "Yes, and it's also about being role models. Our actions speak louder than words. When they see us respecting each other's traditions and beliefs, they learn to do the same."

Sarah said, "I think that's the key. It's about living those values every day."

As they exchanged ideas, they realized that though parenting in a multicultural world is challenging, it also incredibly rewarding. They were not just raising children. They were actually nurturing the next generation of citizens who are going to be compassionate, understanding, and respectful globally.

Sarah felt a swell of admiration. "That's a wonderful approach. It's evident in how they carry themselves. You've managed to blend your cultural values with modern parenting so beautifully."

"It's not always simple, but it's important," Arpita said with a nod. We are assisting them in navigating their true identities in a difficult environment by providing them with a solid foundation and an awareness of their background."

As they talked more about their experiences, it was clear that both families had found strength and unity despite their different cultural upbringings. Their children were growing up with a deep appreciation for diversity and a strong sense of self.

The developed a strong bond between Sarah and Arpita as they both aimed at producing caring and well-rounded kids. They wanted their children to serve as a symbol of understanding, and respect who can celebrate diversity. By working together, they wanted to leave a legacy of acceptance and love for upcoming generations. They wanted to protect their cultural history.

The autumn leaves swirled gently in the cool breeze. Michael and Mr. Chatterjee sat on the Petersons' porch for drinks. The neighborhood was quiet and safe. From a distance, they could hear kids laughing in the park. Michael moved forward to inquire, "Mr. Chatterjee, I've always appreciated the harmony in your family. I'm curious regarding the dynamics of different families. How did you help Arpita to adjust in your family? How did they accept her despite the differences?"

Mr. Chatterjee smiled, "Michael, it wasn't always easy. Yet it was deeply rewarding. You know, Arpita and I come from very different backgrounds, despite the fact that we are both Hindu. My family is Bengali, and we have rich cultural traditions and a great preference for classical music. Arpita, however, grew up in a strict Brahmin family where observance of rituals and vegetarianism was valued highly.

He took a thoughtful sip of his whisky before continuing. “The first step was an open communication. We had long discussions about our beliefs, traditions, and expectations. I made sure my family understood that Arpita comes from a different tradition. However, she shared our core values like respect, kindness, and family unity. I also emphasized the importance of embracing change. I asked them to see it as an opportunity for growth.”

Michael nodded, intrigued. “And how did Arpita feel about it?”

“Initially, she was apprehensive,” Mr. Chatterjee admitted. “But I stood by her side. I assured her that we would blend our traditions in such a way that will honor both of our backgrounds. We found common ground by celebrating festivals together. This, incorporating both our customs. For example, during Durga Puja, Arpita would help with the vegetarian offerings. Gradually my family learned to appreciate the vegetarian dishes she introduced from her traditions.”

Michael smiled, feeling enlightened. “It sounds like the key to your successful marriage is mutual respect and open-mindedness.”

“Absolutely,” Mr. Chatterjee agreed. “It was about creating a sense of belongingness. We respected and valued each other’s differences.

These differences added richness to our lives. We all want to be heard, accepted and appreciated for who we are. That's how you create a family. A family where everyone feels they truly belong to one single unit."

Mr. Chatterjee leaned back in his chair,with a thoughtful expression. "Belongingness is about accepting and being accepted," he said. We have a decision to make. It's a choice we make. It requires effort from both sides. If you want to belong to something or someone, it's important that the individual feels genuinely welcome. This sense of welcome doesn't just happen. It needs to be created intentionally."

Michael nodded, prompting Mr. Chatterjee to elaborate further. "For someone to feel welcome, proper introduction and presentation are required. When Arpita first joined our family, I made sure to open the door appropriately. I introduced her not just as my wife but as a person with her own unique story and background. It was important that my family listened to her, showed interest in her experiences, and understood what she wanted to convey."

He paused, letting the words sink in. "You see, someone must take the initiative to create an environment where the new person feels seen and heard. It's about balancing the act of sharing and receiving. Arpita did her part by sharing her traditions and values, and my family did theirs by being open and respectful."

Michael could see the truth in Mr. Chatterjee's words. "So, it's about creating a space where everyone's story is valued?"

"Exactly," Mr. Chatterjee affirmed. "When Arpita and I decided to get married, we knew that we both have individual stories. We knew that this is what will make us unique. We made a conscious effort to balance our traditions. During our festivals, we made sure to incorporate elements from both our backgrounds. This not only honored our individual cultures but also created a new, shared family tradition."

Michael smiled, feeling enlightened. "It sounds like mutual respect and intentional effort were key in making everyone feel they belong."

"Absolutely," Mr. Chatterjee replied. "True acceptance and gratitude are more important than tolerance in this situation. We cultivate a sense of belonging that improves our family life by establishing an atmosphere where everyone is respected and feels at home."

Michael had new direction in mind while they sipped their beverages. He had learned about the peaceful existence of the Chatterjee family from the chat, and it had also motivated him to take greater care in creating a feeling of community and belonging in his own family.

Chapter 6 -The Unschooling Experiment

Arpita Chatterjee sitting at the kitchen table looked at the latest report card. Her brow furrowed with concern. Raj's grades were dropping. It clearly showed that he was struggling hard, more than ever. Looking at Arpita's worried face Mr. Chatterjee sat next to her.

He put his hand around her shoulder and he asked gently, "What's wrong, Arpita?" Though he already had some idea.

She replied, taking a deep breath. "It's about Raj.His grades have been dropping steadily. I think it's something more than just the studies. He is not comfortable at school. The feeling of not fitting in due to the cultural differences is taking a toll on him."

Mr. Chatterjee nodded. His face showed the same concern. "I too have noticed it. He's been quiet lately. He is not his usual self. What do you think we should do?"

"I've been thinking about homeschooling," Arpita said. "I think he should be given an environment where he feels safe and understood. This traditional schooling isn't working for him right now."

Mr. Chatterjee considered her words. "Don't you think homeschooling is a big decision,Arpita? But if you feel it will make

Raj happier and more comfortable, it's worth considering. Have you thought about how we would manage it?"

Arpita said, her voice gaining strength. "Yes,I've read a lot about different methods of schooling. Home teaching or individual learning might be the future for Raj. According to me, learning is highly personal. Each individual must find out for themselves which learning method will be best. We can tailor his education to suit his needs."

Mr. Chatterjee nodded thoughtfully. "I agree that individual learning has its benefits. Each child has its own unique way of understanding the world around. We can help him to be personally and academically successful by focusing on his strengths and interests. "

Arpita continued, " For his overall development, group training is also important. This will teach him to cooperate with others and understand different perspectives. We can find out ways to make sure that he interacts socially. We can perhaps do this through extracurricular activities or community groups."

"Perfect. That sounds like a balanced approach," Mr. Chatterjee said. "We want Raj not only to be academically successful but also socially competent. Homeschooling might give him the safe space he needs to develop his confidence and love for learning."

Arpita was happy and hopeful for the first time in weeks. "Exactly. We can provide him with a curriculum that suits his learning style. Whether it's project-based learning, hands-on activities, or traditional textbook methods. And we can still involve him in group activities to build his social skills."

Mr. Chatterjee added, "We should also consider hybrid schooling options, where he can attend classes for certain subjects and work from home for others. This way, he gets the best of both worlds—personalized education and social interaction."

Arpita agreed. "We can look into local homeschool groups and online resources. There are many families in similar situations who have found success with homeschooling. It's about finding what works best for Raj."

"We must be adaptable and willing to change our strategies as we go," Mr. Chatterjee stated. "It's important that Raj feels supported and knows that we're doing this for his well-being."

Arpita's eyes brightened with determination. "Yes, we will make sure that he knows that our support is there with him during the entire process. Learning is not a one-size-fits-all process. It's about knowing which path is best for each individual.

They sat together to plan their son's educational future. They felt connected with an understanding about their purpose for their son's future. Their first goal was Raj's success and happiness. They were dedicated to giving him the greatest learning environment they could.

They started looking into hybrid schooling options. They visited various other homeschool families, to review curricula. When they told Raj about the new plan, he felt happy. They noticed that he was excited and hopeful after a long time.

Appreciate his parents' efforts, Raj said quietly. "Thank you dad and mom."

Arpita hugged him tightly and said,"We love you, Raj. We want you to be happy and successful. We are ready to do whatever it takes to make that happen."

Mr. Chatterjee joined the embrace, feeling a deep sense of relief and optimism. Together, they would navigate this new educational journey, supporting Raj in every way possible, ensuring he had the opportunity to learn and grow in an environment that truly suited him.

Mr. Chatterjee sat back, deep in thought. "You know," he began, looking at Arpita with a reflective expression, "this whole discussion about Raj's schooling reminds me of the struggles my cousin, Rohit, faced during his school years. Have you ever faced difficulties with the school system?"

Arpita nodded sympathetically, encouraging him to continue.

"Mass learning has never really been my style," Mr. Chatterjee admitted. "I learned to read and write quite late in life. In fact, I'm writing dyslexic. For me, much of my learning has been about storing knowledge and then seeing and understanding connections between different things."

He paused, recalling his cousin's experiences. "Rohit had it even tougher. The traditional school system has a rigid structure. It is like a one-size-fits-all approach. Due to which it was a constant struggle for him. He was a bright kid. He was full of curiosity and creativity. However, due to his unique learning style, the system could not cater him."

Mr. Chatterjee described how Rohit's teachers frequently misinterpreted him. He was not the kind of student who could read a textbook quietly and retain the knowledge. He needed to interact more directly and practically with the material. Nevertheless, there was little opportunity for individualized instruction or customized teaching strategies in a classroom with thirty or more children."

Arpita listened intently, realizing how similar Raj's situation was to Rohit's. "So what did Rohit do?" she asked.

"Rohit struggled," Mr. Chatterjee continued. "He faced a tough time to keep up with the fast moving syllabus. He was often labeled as inattentive or lazy as he couldn't perform well in written exams. But the truth was, he learned differently. He was more of a listener than a reader. He would record lectures so he could pause and search for facts if there were things he didn't understand."

Mr. Chatterjee sighed, remembering the frustration Rohit felt. "There's no point in going on if you don't understand something, but unfortunately, the system expects students to keep up regardless. Rohit often felt like he was left behind because the teachers couldn't slow down for just one student."

Arpita nodded, empathizing with Rohit's plight. "It must have been so hard for him."

"It was," Mr. Chatterjee agreed. "But Rohit was determined. He found his own ways to learn and succeed. He taught himself to pause and take the time to really understand the material before moving on. This method served him well in the long run, but it was a lonely and challenging journey."

He continued, "Mass education was difficult for Rohit because it didn't allow for individuality in learning styles. He needed a different approach, one that recognized and respected his unique way of processing information. Unfortunately, the school system at that time was not flexible enough to accommodate that."

With a contemplative look on his face, Mr. Chatterjee reclined in his chair. "I learned a lot regarding the value of tailored learning from Rohit's experiences. Since no two people are alike, it's critical to acknowledge and support each person's special talents and requirements."

Arpita gave him a knowing glance as she stared at him. She muttered, "That's why we're thinking of homeschooling Raj." "All of us wish to offer him the chance to acquire an approach that works for him most effectively, without feeling compelled to agree to a strict system."

Mr. Chatterjee nodded. "Exactly. It's about finding out what suits him best. Eventually, Rohit found his way, but it took a lot of perseverance and resilience. We need to assist Raj in discovering a better path now. I don't want him to go through the same hardships."

He paused, then added,"The process of learning deserves to be a rewarding and fulfilling moment instead of a cause of stress and frustration," he said after pausing. We're giving Raj the best chance to succeed by thinking about homeschooling, hybrid education, or any other approach that enables him to learn at his own pace and in his own way."

Arpita smiles, finding her motivation restored. Then, she said, "We're doing the right thing." "We'll assist Raj in every manner that we can and make he understands that his distinctive method of gaining knowledge is appreciated and respected."

Mr. Chatterjee agreed, "Yes, we'll give him an environment that makes him feel safe and understood. We will encourage him to explore his interests and talents. Just like Rohit found his way, Raj will too—with our support and love."

The conversation about Rohit's struggles had reinforced their decision. They understood there were other ways to happiness and success except attending school in a traditional way. They were certain that by concentrating on Raj's unique requirements and preferred method of learning, they could assist him in navigating his academic path more easily and confidently.

"Let's start researching more about homeschooling and other flexible learning methods," Arpita suggested. "We need to be well-prepared to make the best decision for Raj."

Mr. Chatterjee nodded, feeling a sense of determination. "We'll do whatever it takes to ensure Raj's success and happiness. Just like Rohit, he'll find his way—with a little guidance and a lot of love."

As they sat together, planning the next steps for Raj's education, they felt a renewed sense of hope and purpose. They knew that by prioritizing Raj's unique learning needs, they were giving him the best chance to thrive and succeed, just as Rohit had eventually done. With their unwavering support and love, Raj would find his path and flourish in a way that suited him best.

Michael and Mr. Chatterjee were sitting on the Petersons' porch. They were enjoying the soft evening air that was rustling the leaves. The conversation shifted into the subject of schooling since Arpita was worried about Raj's declining grades. She was also stressed about his discomfort in the classroom.

Mr. Chatterjee started, "You know, Michael, Arpita and I have been seriously thinking about homeschooling for Raj. His efforts and self-esteem are suffering as a result of the cultural disparities at his school."

Michael nodded thoughtfully. "I've heard that homeschooling can be quite effective for some kids. What brought you to this decision?"

Mr. Chatterjee sighed. "Raj is an intelligent child, but he finds it difficult to learn in a typical classroom. His inability to learn is being impacted by his sense of alienation. We believe that homeschooling could offer him a more personalized and comfortable learning environment."

Michael leaned forward, intrigued. "Tell me more about how you plan to approach it."

Mr. Chatterjee smiled. "We think that education focuses on being able to communicate what you know, not just about gaining knowledge. It's all about figuring out what strategies suit your learning style the best. Raj needs a more individualized approach, something that mass education can't provide."

"Yes, mass education has benefits, but it's not a one-size-fits-all solution," Michael concurred. My cousin went through a similar situation at school. Due to his dyslexia, he had difficulty writing and reading. Traditional methods didn't help him much."

That's exactly it, according to Mr. Chatterjee. Raj need a setting that allows him to learn in a manner that works for him and at his own speed. Our goal is to develop a program that takes use of his interests and strengths.

Michael gave a nod. "How then are you going to strike a balance between the importance of social skills and the need for individual learning?"

"It's a thoughtful question," Mr. Chatterjee answered. "We'll make sure Raj has lots of chances to socialize with other children while homeschooling by offering him, extracurricular activities, and neighborhood groups.Group learning is important for developing cooperation and social skills, but the core academics will be personalized to his needs."

"Sounds like a solid plan," Michael said. "But how will you explain to Raj the importance of education? It's crucial that he understands why you're doing this."

"Without a doubt," Mr. Chatterjee replied. "We'll discuss with him how knowledge is an important thing in life and it helps you to communicate well. We'll tell him that if he puts proper effort, the better he will get.
Isn't that true for each and every one of us? We get more skilled the more we put into our education and abilities."

Michael smiled. "That's true for all of us, isn't it? The more we invest in our education and skills, the more proficient we become."

'Indeed," Mr. Chatterjee remarked. "We want Raj to know that no one is superior to anybody else. Everyone has special talents. It all comes down to identifying your strengths and investing your best in it."
Michael lost in deep thoughts. "Children should understand that their worth is only from just their academic achievements. They must realize that a wide variety of abilities and skills are required by society."

"That's right," Mr. Chatterjee stated. "Raj that he is an important member of the community. He needs to understand that his efforts are valued. We'll support him in pursuing his passions and help him discover the importance of education as the foundation of all he wishes to achieve.

Michael nodded and added, "So, you're basically guiding him to discover his path in life."

“Exactly,” Mr. Chatterjee answered. Education doesn't only teach children facts. It also develops a love of learning. It even assists them in acquiring the abilities necessary to thrive in life.”

Michael smiled. "I think that's an excellent strategy. Children should understand that education is a tool, not merely something they must do, to help them achieve their dreams.

Mr. Chatterjee agreed. “We’ll also explain to Raj that understanding his own abilities and limitations is crucial. He needs to know that it’s okay to struggle with certain things. It doesn’t make him any less capable. Everyone learns at their own pace and have different style of learning.”

“Absolutely,” Michael said. “And by personalizing his education, you’re giving him the best chance to thrive.”

Chatterjee gave a nod. “We'll empower him to take charge of his education. We ask him to experiment with different topics, and to discover what interests him. And we will always be there to help him along the journey.

Michael looked thoughtful. "It's crucial to teach children to appreciate diversity. He needs to collaborate and respect the social aspects of education."

“Certainly,” Mr. Chatterjee said. "We'll make sure that Raj gets lots of chances to interact with other kids. He will be able to understand the importance of empathy and teamwork.”

“So, how do you think you’ll handle the curriculum?” Michael asked.

“We’ll start with a basic structure that covers the core subjects,” Mr. Chatterjee explained. “But we’ll adapt it to Raj’s interests and learning style. We’ll use a mix of traditional textbooks, online resources, and hands-on projects.”

Michael nodded approvingly. “That sounds very comprehensive. And what about assessments?”

“We’ll use a combination of methods,” Mr. Chatterjee said. “Standardized tests where necessary, but also project-based assessments and regular feedback to track his progress.”

“It sounds like you’ve thought this through,” Michael said. “I’m sure Raj will thrive with this approach.”

"Hopefully," Mr. Chatterjee uttered. "All we want is the best opportunity for him to thrive and develop a love of learning." "And that's the most crucial factor,"

Michael agreed. "You'll have him set for life if you can inculcate a love of learning."

For a brief while, the two men sat in a comfortable silence and thought back on the importance of their chat.

Michael broke the silence. “You know, I think this conversation has helped me see things differently too. Maybe we should look at more individualized ways to support our kids’ education as well.”

Mr. Chatterjee smiled. “Education is a journey for the entire family. It’s about looking for the best for each child and supporting them in their growth.”

Michael nodded. “Absolutely. Thanks for sharing your thoughts with me. It’s given me a lot to think about.”

Michael got a pat on the back from Mr. Chatterjee. "Anytime, my friend. We are all working toward giving our children the greatest life possible.”

The two friends relaxed as the twilight sky took on pink and orange hues. They felt confident that they were in the correct direction for securing their childrens’ futures. Regardless of how dissimilar those pathways might appear.

*****

Arpita and Sarah sat in the living room while Michael and Mr. Chatterjee carried on their conversation in the porch. The room was nice and inviting thanks to the fireplace's soothing light. It improved the two women's sense of closeness and trust in one another.

After filling china cups with tea, Sarah gave one to Arpita.She began with a thoughtful look on her face. I overheard some of the conversation between our husbands. It's interesting to know how each of us view education and future plans for our kids from a different angle.

Taking a sip of her tea, Arpita nodded. 'No doubt. When it comes to making plans for our children's futures, we have a lot to take into account."

Arpita reclined back in the couch and took a deep breath. It's a complicated problem. On the one hand, we want to provide our kids with the greatest chances possible.
As we want them to be successful and happy. On the other hand, we sometimes worry that too much planning can stop their ability to make their own choices and it may even hinder their individuality."

Sarah nodded her head in agreement. "I think it's about finding a balance. Planning can provide structure and guidance. But it is also crucial to leave room for the child's own interests and passions to emerge."

Arpita smiled. "Exactly. I wanted Raj to excel in his studies and participate in extracurricular activities. I wanted him to be an all rounder. I had all these plans for him when he was 5-6 years. But as he grew older, I realized that some of my plans didn't match with his interests."

Sarah leaned in, intrigued. "How did you handle that?"

"Well," Arpita said, "I had to let go of my preconceived notions. I really listened to Raj. Right from the age of 7, he knew what he wanted. Since then, he has been passionate about art and music. While I hadn't initially considered these areas as part of his 'future success'. Once I acknowledged his interests, I saw him flourish in ways I had not even imagined."

Sarah smiled warmly. "That's wonderful, Arpita. I too believe that it is important to let our children walk on their own paths to some extent."

With her vision reflecting the warmth of the fire Arpita nodded. "Yes, and I believe that giving children a range of alternatives and letting them make their own decisions is equally important. Parents who overplan in extensive detail without taking their child's preferences into account may find themselves frustrated and unmotivated."

"Absolutely," Sarah agreed. "It's similar to providing them with the means to construct their future. It is even about letting them choose how to employ those means."

Taking a deep breath, Arpita felt a connection with Sarah. 'And, is it not more than just an issue of education? It concerns their general happiness and well-being. Teaching people to accept accountability for their decisions and draw lessons from past experiences is the goal."

Sarah put down her cup on the side table. "It is true. As their parents, it is our responsibility to guide, encourage, and provide them the chance to learn and develop. But in the end, they must have the confidence to choose for themselves."

Arpita's thoughts took her back to her early years in India. "You know, Sarah, I was raised in a traditional home where my future was predetermined. There was very little space to deviate from my parents' strict expectations. It was only after I married Mr. Chatterjee and moved abroad that I realized the importance of having choices."

Sarah listened intently, appreciating the insight into Arpita's background. "That must have been a significant shift for you."

"It was," Arpita admitted. "And I've made an effort to keep Raj in mind when doing this. I don't want our expectations to make him feel limited. I wish him to be free to follow his own path and pursue his passions."

Sarah smiled. "You seem to be doing a fantastic job," Raj is fortunate to have parents who are so forgiving and encouraging."

Arpita blushed slightly at the compliment. “Thank you, Sarah. I think we all try our best, don’t we?”

Sarah nodded. “We do. And it helps to have friends who understand and share similar values.”

After discussing many aspects of parenting, Sarah opened up about her own interactions with her children. As she put it, "Finding the right balance is not always easy. For example, my daughter is good at science but not so good at arithmetic. It has come to my attention that it is acceptable for her to possess both strengths and shortcomings. What’s important is that she enjoys learning and feels supported.”

Arpita agreed. “Yes, we often put so much pressure on our children to excel in everything. But it’s okay for them to have areas where they need more help. It’s all part of their growth.”

The conversation continued naturally as the evening went on. They had covered a wide range of topics like parenting and educational subjects. Their conversation gave both women the feeling of relief and recognition. Knowing they weren't the only ones with these worries and that they might benefit from one another's experiences was consoling.

Michael and Mr. Chatterjee were finishing off their own chat back on the porch. "You've provided me with ample material for contemplation," grinned Michael as he shook his head. "I may need to reconsider our approach to our children's education."

Mr. Chatterjee chuckled. "I think we're all constantly reevaluating. Parenting is a journey, and we're learning as much as our children are."

Michael nodded. "Absolutely. Thanks for the insights. It's been a valuable discussion."

As the evening drew to a close, the two families felt a renewed sense of connection and support. They were grateful for the opportunity to share their thoughts and learn from one another.

The next day, as Sarah visited Arpita to express her admiration for the previous day's festivities, she couldn't help but marvel at the intricate decorations and the seamless flow of events. "The arrangements and planning were fantastic," Sarah praised warmly.

Arpita smiled, her eyes gleaming with pride. "It wasn't my plan; it was the children's idea," she revealed. Sarah felt a swell of pride and told Arpita, "You've raised them so well. Your parenting style is truly admirable."

The two families' mutual respect and understanding were reaffirmed by this brief conversation. It served as a monument to the value of a strong sense of community, mutual learning, and support amongst people navigating the difficulties of parenthood.

The Petersons and the Chatterjees kept exchanging stories and ideas throughout the ensuing weeks. They talked about the value of striking a balance between structure and freedom, investigated various teaching philosophies, and encouraged one another to provide their kids the best possible care.

The choice to think about homeschooling Raj was a big one for Arpita and Mr. Chatterjee. They were determined to find the greatest strategy for their son's requirements even though they knew it wouldn't be simple. They looked into different homeschooling curricula, talked to other parents who had made the same decision, and made plans for Raj to continue having lots of social connections.

In the meantime, Sarah and Michael also started to consider their own parenting style more carefully. They came to understand the value of adaptability and the necessity of changing their approaches to fit the individual learning preferences of each kid.

As the two families worked through these difficulties together, their relationship grew closer. They discovered that while making plans for the future is crucial, it's also critical to keep an open mind and follow their children's unique needs and interests.

The Petersons and the Chatterjees learned via their common experience that listening, adapting, and assisting their kids in forging their own paths are the true measures of effective parenting rather than strict planning. They discovered that education is about more than simply helping students succeed academically; it's also about creating a passion of learning, stimulating curiosity, and assisting their kids in developing into self-assured, well-rounded people.

Through their shared journey, the Petersons and the Chatterjees discovered that the essence of good parenting lies not in rigid planning, but in the ability to listen, adapt, and support their children in finding their own paths. They learned that education is not just about academic achievement, but about fostering a love for learning, encouraging curiosity, and helping their children become confident, well-rounded individuals.

They were filled with immense thankfulness and joy as they saw their kids flourish. They understood that by cooperating, honoring one another's viewpoints, and lending support to other people, they were fostering a loving environment in which their kids might grow and thrive.

Ultimately, that friendship between the Chatterjees and the Petersons developed into a lovely illustration of how different families can unite, exchange knowledge, and build a better future for their offspring. Through their journey, they discovered that the real meaning of parenting isn't found in planning; rather, it's found in the love, understanding, and support parents give to their kids along the route.

Chapter 7 - The Cyberbully

Sarah and Michael were sitting in the living room, enjoying a quiet evening after dinner. However, their peace was interrupted by the sight of their son, Ethan. He seemed unusually anxious. He was hunched over his laptop. His face illuminated the blue light of the screen. Every now and then, he would glance nervously around the room. At the same time, his fingers tapping restlessly on the keyboard.

Michael nudged Sarah and nodded towards Ethan. "I have been observing him for the past few days. Since then, I have seen him like that. Do you think something is troubling him?"

Sarah raised her brows out of concern. "Yes, I've noticed it too. He seems to be preoccupied. Let us talk to him."

As they came near Ethan, he quickly minimized his screen and looked up. His eyes widened with surprise. "Hey, buddy," Michael said gently. "Is everything okay? You seem a bit tense."

Ethan tried to push a smile. "I'm fine, Dad. It is just that I have a lot of schoolwork."

Sarah wasn't convinced. "Ethan, feel free to share with us if anything is bothering you. You know that you can discuss anything with us, right?"

Ethan was hesitant. Biting his lip, he said, "It's nothing, for sure."

Michael and Sarah were worried. “"Ethan, you know that we're here to help you," Michael said in a tone that was both firm and compassionate.

Ethan,” Michael said, in a very firm but kind voice, “you know, we’re here to help you. Is someone bothering you online?”

Ethan’s eyes widened slightly, and he looked down, his silence speaking volumes.

Sarah’s heart sank. “Ethan, have you been experiencing cyberbullying?”

Tears filled Ethan's eyes as he looked up. "Mom, I'm not sure," Ethan said. "There are these students at school who have been making fun of me and sending me nasty messages online."

Sarah and Michael were angry and felt sad. Sarah put her arms around Ethan and said, "You don't need to deal with this alone. We're here to support you during this.”

Michael nodded in agreement. “Let us see what these messages are. We will see what we can do.”

They spent the next hour going through Ethan’s online accounts, identifying the bullies and saving the evidence. As they worked, Michael turned to Sarah. "This is the issue with technology and social media. This has always been our concern. It's so simple for kids to hide behind devices and act so cruelly.

Sarah nodded, her face serious. "The ease with which kids might get caught in these kinds of circumstances is terrifying. They seem very innocent and young.

Michael sighed. "We need to have a serious talk about the rise of social media and technology, and how to handle it. Not just for Ethan, but for all of us."

Sarah agreed. "Absolutely. We must discuss the many kinds of connections that might develop online as well as any possible repercussions. Ethan must learn to spot reliable information sources and know when he is being manipulated."

Michael sat next to Sarah, and they continued to concentrate on Ethan. He was clearly more at ease now. He knew his parents were supporting him. "The internet may be a wonderful tool for learning and connecting with others. However, people with bad intentions can easily take advantage of others using it," Michael stated.

Sarah continued, "We must instill the value of source control, in Ethan and the other children. They must be able to distinguish between trustworthy and untrustworthy information, as well as recognize that various online groups have distinct goals."

Feeling his parents' worry, Ethan questioned, "But how do I know whom to trust?"

Michael looked his son in the eye. "Ethan, it's not always that easy. However, you may begin by limiting your interactions to those you actually know. Be aware of strangers, your so-called online friends. They thrive to become your friend. You should avoid them. And don't hesitate to come to us if something or someone bothers you."

"We want you to establish certain guidelines for your online activities," Sarah continued. It is crucial to maintain an appropriate equilibrium between your virtual and real life. Overuse of the internet might make it more difficult to recognize the warning signs of such harmful behavior."

Ethan nodded, absorbing their advice. "Okay, I'll be more careful. And I promise I'll come to you if anything happens again."

Sarah hugged him tightly. "That's all we ask, Ethan. We're here to protect you and guide you."

Michael took a deep breath. "I now understand how crucial it is that we continue to be active in your online activities as a result of this circumstance. We must maintain open lines of contact and provide you regular updates on our progress."

Sarah agreed. "And it goes beyond simple observation. You must learn from us how to utilize the internet sensibly and securely. Although it's a strong tool, there are some risks that you should be aware of."

Ethan felt a mixture of thankfulness and relief as he turned to face his parents. "Thank you, Dad and Mom. Knowing that you are here to assist makes me feel a lot better."

The family kept discussing the effects of social media and technology as the evening went on. They talked about how important it is to understand and clarify the various kinds of relationships that can develop online and how to spot dishonest or manipulative behavior.

Michael brought up the importance of source control again. "Ethan, it is crucial to have information about the person with whom you're interacting online. Not everything you read on the internet is true. Always check the source of the information. If you are not convinced, cross-reference with other reliable sources."

Sarah added, "And remember, different groups online have different goals. Some might be trying to sell you something. While there might be others who want to push their goals. Don't take everything at the face value. Be critical of what you read."

Ethan nodded, taking their advice to heart. "I understand. I'll be more careful and always come to you. I promise to be extra careful and to consult you whenever I have any doubts."

The family felt united and understanding as the evening came to an end. They were determined to face the continuous task of managing the world of technology and social networking sites together. Even though they knew it would not be easy. After Ethan had been put to bed, Michael and Sarah expressed their gratitude for the chance to talk about this crucial matter.

Michael and Sarah put Ethan to sleep. They felt grateful for the opportunity to address this important issue. They understood that with their involvement and by maintaining open communication, they could help Ethan and their other children navigate the digital world safely and responsibly.

Following up, Michael and Sarah kept teaching Ethan about internet safety. They talked about privacy settings, the value of protecting personal data, and the best ways to report and block abusive users. In order to maintain a good balance between his online and offline lives. They also urged him to engage in offline hobbies and activities.

Feeling stronger and more encouraged, Ethan started to view the internet more critically. He became aware of the signs and symptoms of cyberbullying. He realised that his parents were always there to support him.

The event strengthened the bonds between the family members. It also emphasized how crucial it is to remain aware and watchful in the digital age. They were aware that by cooperating, they could overcome the difficulties associated with social.

In the end, the Peterson family understood that the best way to handle the rise of social media and technology was education, communication, and support. By developing a culture of openness and understanding, they could help their children use the internet with confidence and resilience.

The Petersons and the Chatterjees were spending a nice afternoon in the backyard over the weekend. The grownups were conversing and having iced tea as the youngsters played. Sarah observed that, considering the volatile circumstances they were living in, their conversations frequently returned to social issues and current affairs.

"Ben has been asking a lot of questions about what's going on in the world. How do you and Arpita discuss social issues with your kids?" Michael turning his face towards Mr. Chatterjee asked.

Mr. Chatterjee smiled thoughtfully. "It requires careful balancing. We think that rather than overloading children with information that they cannot alter, we should give them just enough knowledge to make them aware. We focus on issues that they can relate to and understand."

Arpita nodded in agreement. "We start by discussing the importance of belonging and community at home. If they understand the foundations of respect, empathy, and responsibility within our family, they can apply those values to the wider world."

Sarah leaned forward and asked, "So, you start with the basics at home and then go on to larger issues?"

"Exactly," Arpita replied. "We limit exposure to news that could be distressing or confusing. Instead, we encourage conversations about problems they might encounter in their daily life. The issues like bullying or environmental concerns. We talk about how they can make a difference in those areas."

Michael nodded. "That's a good approach. We've had trouble deciding how much knowledge to give Ethan. While we don't want to totally isolate him. At the same time we also do not want them to feel helpless."

Mr. Chatterjee added, "Teaching them how to differentiate between information they can rely with and data that's simply out of their control is one important thing. We empower our children to focus on what they can change, like being kind to others or participating in community clean-ups."

Sarah smiled, "We try to do the same. We encourage Ethan to get involved in activities where he can make a tangible difference. It helps him feel more in control and positive about his role in society."

Arpita added, "Exactly. When discussing current events, we make it clear that while he might not be able to solve global issues, he can still have a significant impact locally. It's about creating a sense of empowerment rather than despair."

Michael reflected on this. "So, you steer conversations towards actionable topics and local involvement?"

"Yes," Mr. Chatterjee affirmed. "We also emphasize critical thinking. We teach Raj to question the sources of his information and understand different perspectives. It's not about shielding him from reality but about guiding him to think constructively."

Sarah asked, "What about social media? It's such a big part of kids' lives now."

Arpita sighed. "Social media is tricky. We monitor his usage and talk about the difference between real life and what people post online. We stress the importance of not comparing himself to others and to always verify the information before accepting it as truth."

Mr. Chatterjee continued, "We also encourage Raj to discuss what he sees online with us. If something confuses or worries him, we talk about it together. It's about creating an open dialogue."

Michael agreed. "We've noticed that open communication helps Ethan feel more secure. He knows he can come to us with anything, and we'll listen without judgment."

Arpita smiled, "That's key. Children need to feel that their thoughts and concerns are valid. It builds trust and helps them navigate the complexities of the world."

Mr. Chatterjee added, "And it's not just about problems. We also discuss positive events and achievements around the world. It's important to show them that there's good happening too."

Sarah looked thoughtful. "So, it's a balance of protecting them, informing them, and empowering them to make a difference?"

"Exactly," Arpita said. "And also teaching them to be critical thinkers. They should learn to question and analyze information rather than just accepting it at face value."

Leaning back, Michael soaked it all in. Though it requires a lot of thought, the subject is crucial. Although the world may appear overwhelming, youngsters can develop into thoughtful, self-assured adults if we raise them well."

Sarah smiled at the Chatterjees. "I am grateful to you for sharing your insights. It's comforting to know we're all trying our best to raise our kids."

Mr. Chatterjee nodded in agreement. "Absolutely. It's great to have friends like you with whom we can share our thoughts and problems in this journey of parenthood."

The two families connected more deeply while the kids played together because they knew they were working towards the same goal of helping their kids navigate a world that was getting more complicated. They had come away from the talk with fresh ideas and a renewed resolve to empower their kids and maintain honest lines of communication.

As they prepared to depart later that night, Michael turned to face Mr. Chatterjee. "One last thing – how do you handle it when your children come home upset about something they saw or heard?"

Mr. Chatterjee paused thoughtfully. "We try to create a safe space for him to express his feelings. We listen without interrupting, and then we discuss ways to process those emotions. Sometimes, we use those moments as teaching opportunities to discuss empathy and resilience."

Sarah added, "We do something similar with Ethan. We let him know it's okay to feel upset. We help him understand why he feels that way. Then we talk about different constructive ways to cope."

Arpita smiled. "We seem to be in agreement with each other. It all comes down to lovingly and empathetically mentoring them as they develop into wise, caring adults."

The Petersons and Chatterjees experienced a sense of purpose and solidarity as they said goodbye. Their friendship had become stronger as well as their parenting techniques. It is all because of their discussions about current affairs and social issues. They were aware that they could overcome the difficulties of parenting in this complicated world when they stood together. They can impart virtues of empowerment, empathy, and critical thinking in their children by standing together and sharing their experiences. It all comeown to lovingly and empathetically mentoring them as they develop into wise, caring adults."

The Chatterjees and Petersons had come to their neighborhood for a party. The sound of kids laughing and the aroma of grilled food blended together. As the evening progressed, Mr. Chatterjee and Michael managed to find a quiet space where they could talk about the social and academic difficulties their children were facing.

Michael turned to Mr. Chatterjee and asked, "Have you had any difficulties relating to peer pressure or bullying? It seems like such a pervasive issue these days."

Mr. Chatterjee nodded slowly, his expression thoughtful. "Yes, I have. I experienced a lot of exclusion as a child. Peer pressure was a common occurrence. I was frequently shunned by people for choosing to follow my own path. I consider myself to be a path creator—someone who forges ahead where others have failed. Although difficult, it helped to shape who I am now."

Michael paid close attention, feeling that there was more to the tale. "I was different from my peers when I was in school," Mr. Chatterjee went on. I had a distinct viewpoint on the world and a variety of hobbies. I had strong feelings about topics that other people found incomprehensible or unimportant. This made me a target for bullying. There were times when I felt deeply isolated because I didn't fit into the traditional mould that society had set."

He paused and took a sip of his tea, then carried on. Peer pressure is an effective tool. People may find themselves acting in ways they wouldn't normally do. It is an attempt to fit in or stop being teased. I remember the times when my friends teased me for not wearing the newest fashions or for doing things they thought to be "uncool." But I stood firm in my beliefs and interests. I didn't let their opinions dictate my actions."

Michael nodded. "That must have been tough. How did you handle it?"

Mr. Chatterjee smiled slightly. "It was difficult, but my uniqueness gave me strength. I realised early on that I really didn't want to alter who I was to make myself more acceptable to others. I put my hobbies and passions first, even if it means spending time alone myself sometimes. I became resilient and had an intense sense of self throughout time. I discovered the importance of being myself and how to set aside other people's judgments of me."

He went on, "I also had a few mentors and friends who were really encouraging. They helped me to remain true to who I am. They made it clear that uniqueness is acceptable. I needed this support system to help me deal with the difficulties of bullying and peer pressure."

Mr. Chatterjee's self-awareness and resilience impressed Michael. "That is incredibly motivating. What impact do you believe your upbringing has had on your parenting style?

Mr. Chatterjee sat on the chair and raised a query. "I am fully aware of the challenges my children may face from my experiences. Without compromising their uniqueness, I intend to make sure that children receive the tools and support they require to get past these challenges. Arpita and I try to encourage children to follow their passions even if they are different from what other people are doing and to make them feel good about themselves. We instil in them the value of resilience and self-respect."

He continued. "We instill in them the values that being different is acceptable as well as they should never feel pressured to blend in by doing what others say. In addition, we teach children empathy and compassion, which empowers children to voice out against bullying and support their peers."

Michael nodded in agreement. "It's so important for children to have that support. We try to do the same with Ethan. We support him in being authentic and defending his beliefs. We want him to know that he is valued for who he is, not for fitting into a certain mold, even though it isn't always easy."

The two men watched their children play for a while while they sat in cozy silence. Michael then asked, "Have you ever had to intervene directly when Raj faced bullying or peer pressure?"

Mr. Chatterjee sighed. "Indeed, there have been a handful of such cases. Raj experienced bullying as a child due to his cultural heritage and accent. It broke my heart to watch him suffer. In addition to addressing the matter with the school administration, we made sure that Raj was supported at home. We comforted him that he wasn't alone and pushed him to share his experiences."

He continued, "We also enrolled him in activities where they could meet like-minded kids and build their confidence. Over time, Raj learned to stand up for himself and others. He has developed into a vocal opponent of bullying and frequently speaks up when he witnesses someone being mistreated."

Feeling a sense of solidarity with Mr. Chatterjee, Michael smiled. "It sounds like you've done an incredible job raising them. It's so important for kids to have that support system."

Mr. Chatterjee nodded. "Thank you, Michael. It all comes down to establishing a space where people feel respected, secure, and in control. Bullying and peer pressure present serious obstacles, but with the correct help, our kids can overcome them and come out stronger."

The two families sat down to supper as the sun began to set, their relationships deepened by their mutual understanding and discussion. The Petersons and Chatterjee understood that parents could assist their kids face the challenges of growing up with courage and fortitude if they helped one another out and created a welcoming and resilient atmosphere.

"Michael, I've been thinking a lot about empathy and social duty," Mr. Chatterjee started as they enjoyed their drinks. "How do you teach Ethan about these values?"

Michael nodded thoughtfully. "We try to lead by example. Sarah and I always show kindness to others. We talk about our actions and how they affect people around us."

"That's important," Mr. Chatterjee agreed. "I believe empathy starts with understanding oneself. If you know your feelings, you can understand others better."

Michael leaned in. "How do you explain that to Raj?"

Mr. Chatterjee smiled. "We have conversations about emotions. If Raj feels sad or angry, we talk about why. Only when he understands his own feelings will he be able to relate to others. It's a step-by-step process."

Michael nodded. "That makes sense. We also try doing something similar with Ethan. We also involve him in activities that teach empathy, like volunteering."

Mr. Chatterjee said, "That's a great idea. We should do more of that. It's a way to show that duty isn't just a responsibility, but an opportunity to help."

"Exactly," Michael replied. "When Ethan sees us helping others, he learns that it's part of being a good person. We want him to see duty as a chance to make a difference."

Mr. Chatterjee looked thoughtful. "We also discuss social issues at home. We explain that everyone has a role in society. It's not just about fitting in, but contributing positively."

Michael smiled. "We do that too. We talk about fairness and justice. It's important for them to understand that their actions can impact the larger community."

Mr. Chatterjee nodded. "Yes, and it's also about giving them the tools to act. We teach Raj to stand up for what's right, even if it's difficult."

"That's crucial," Michael agreed. "Ethan had a situation at school with bullying. We explained that it's his duty to support his friends and speak up against wrong."

"How did he handle it?" Mr. Chatterjee asked.

"He did well," Michael said proudly. "He told the teacher and stood by his friend. It was a big lesson for him in empathy and duty."

"That's inspiring," Mr. Chatterjee said. "It shows that teaching these values at home can really make a difference."

Michael nodded. "We also try to limit exposure to negative influences. Social media can sometimes distort their views. We focus on real-life experiences and discussions."

"Absolutely," Mr. Chatterjee agreed. "We do the same. It's about building a solid foundation. If they understand their own roles, they'll see their duties as opportunities."

The two fathers shared a moment of understanding, their conversation underscoring the importance of guiding their children in empathy and social duty.

Meanwhile, inside the house, Sarah and Arpita were having a similar discussion.

"Arpita, you've done an amazing job with Raj and Priya," Sarah said. "They're so considerate and aware of others' feelings."

"Thank you, Sarah," Arpita replied. "We try our best. It's important to teach them empathy from a young age."

Sarah nodded. "Absolutely. We involve Ethan in community activities. It helps him see the bigger picture and understand his role in society."

Arpita smiled. "That's wonderful. We talk a lot about emotions at home. If they understand their own feelings, they can relate better to others."

"Exactly," Sarah agreed. "We also encourage Ethan to be curious about others. Asking questions and listening is a big part of empathy."

"True," Arpita said. "We also emphasise the importance of kindness in everyday actions. Small gestures can have a big impact."

Sarah leaned in. "How do you handle social duty with Raj and Priya?"

"We involve them in decisions," Arpita explained. "When we do something for the community, we explain why it's important. It's not just a task, but a way to contribute."

"That's a great approach," Sarah said. "We do something similar. We want Ethan to see duty as a positive thing, not just a chore."

"Exactly," Arpita replied. "We also talk about social issues at home. It's important for them to understand fairness and justice."

Sarah nodded. “We do that too. We want Ethan to understand that his actions can make a difference. It’s about empowering them to act.”

Arpita smiled. “Yes, and it’s about giving them the confidence to stand up for what’s right.”

Sarah agreed. “This journey is worth travelling. To make them become compassionate adults, I think teaching them empathy and social duty will be a great help.”

As the barbecue continued, the two families shared more ideas and experiences, strengthening their resolve to raise empathetic and socially responsible children.

Chapter 8 -The Activist Family

The Chatterjees and Petersons made the decision to volunteer at a nearby food bank on Saturday. The cold weather permeated the air, and the spirit of families banding jointly to support their town was palpable. Since it was the very first time any family had brought their kids to volunteer, this day was very memorable.

Upon reaching the food bank, the kids were excited and inquisitive. This was a place that Raj, Anika, Ben and Ethan had never gone before. They turned to observe the food piles, the humming volunteers, and the folks entering to receive help. After gathering their kids, Mr. Chatterjee and Michael started to explain the significance of what they were going to accomplish.

"Today, we're here to support those who need it," Michael remarked as he bent to meet the children's eyes. It is our responsibility to ensure that those who lack sufficient food have access to food. It's how we return the favor to the community."

"This represents what social responsibility means," Mr. Chatterjee continued. It's about looking out for one another and ensuring that everyone has access to the necessities for a healthy lifestyle. It's about everybody around us, not just about us."

The children nodded, their eyes wide with understanding. They followed their parents into the food bank and were assigned various tasks. Ethan and Raj were put in charge of sorting canned goods, while Priya helped to pack boxes of food.

As they worked, Sarah and Arpita explained the significance of their actions. "By doing this, you're making a real difference," Sarah told them. "The food you pack today will go to families who might otherwise go hungry. You're helping them get through tough times."

Arpita added, "This is what it means to be part of a community. We help each other because we care. And when we do, we create a better place for everyone to live."

The children listened intently as they worked. They began to see the worth of their dedication, no matter how small. They were proud about what they had been doing and could see the thanks in the expressions of those who visited the food bank.

They took some time off after working hard for a few hours. The families sat together, sharing snacks and reflecting on their experience. Priya spoke up first, "I didn't know so many people needed help. I'm glad we came."

Raj nodded in agreement. "Yeah, it feels good to help. I want to do this more often."

Ethan looked thoughtful. "We should tell our friends about this. Maybe they can help too."

Michael smiled at his son. "That's a great idea, Ethan. The more people who help, the better. You can make a big difference by spreading the word."

Sarah added, "And it's not just about today. Social responsibility is something we carry with us every day. Whether it is volunteering, showing kindness to others, or sticking up for what is right, it is about making decisions that benefit other people."

Both the families left the food bank at the end of the day, their purpose revitalized. The kids couldn't wait to tell their pals about their experience and encourage them to join part. They learned the value of social duty from the event, and it also stoked their desire to change the world.

On their way back home, Mr. Chatterjee recalled the day's events. “It was a great time together. Serving as a volunteer team has strengthened our bond as a family. It serves as a reminder of our ability to create a positive change.”

Michael agreed. "Absolutely. Now, our children will remember this lesson for the rest of their lives. They have understood that, no matter how small their actions might look, they can have an impact."

Arpita smiles as she looks at her children in the rearview mirror. "This was only the start. We can contact so many more individuals and provide assistance in so many different ways."

Sarah added, "And we will. One step at a time, we'll teach our children the value of empathy and the importance of social duty."

The Petersons and Chatterjees continued to volunteer regularly, each experience reinforcing the lessons of empathy and social responsibility. They watched with pride as their children grew into compassionate, aware, and active members of their community. Through their actions, they demonstrated that true change begins at home and that each person has the power to make a difference.

The Chatterjees and the Petersons had formed a close bond over the years. Despite this, they were from different cultural backgrounds. They shared common values of family and community. After a long day of volunteering at the local food bank, the two families gathered in the Petersons' living room. The children played games and enjoyed their time together. The adults sat around, sipping hot tea. They started to discuss the difficulties of raising children in today's world.

Mr. Chatterjee tested his back on the couch, he took a deep breath. "One of my biggest worries is about the people who always surround our children. I'm always concerned that they might not be suitable role models for them."

Michael understood his concern. “I can totally relate to it. My concern is not just about the people they meet at school or in the neighborhood. It’s also about being influenced by the internet. The people whom they connect to on social media, and through other media.”

Arpita, sitting beside Mr. Chatterjee added, “I am worried about the pressure our children might feel to fit in or to conform to behaviors and attitudes that don’t align with our family values. On seeing others having different conditions or lifestyles, they might develop their own guilt.”

Sarah remarked, "It's really an excellent line to walk, isn't it? We want our children to be open minded as well as accepted by others. We desire to make sure they uphold the morals we have instilled in them.”

Mr. Chatterjee gave a thoughtful nod. That's right. It may be difficult to control what they are exposed to. Yet we can guide and assist them in making wise decisions.

Michael also agreed. "For this reason, it's important that we communicate openly with our children. We must discuss with them about the things they observe and hear. This will help them to know between what's good and what's wrong.

Arpita smiled. “And for that we need to lead by example. If they see us being kind, respectful, and true to our values, they’ll be more likely to follow in our footsteps.”

Sarah leaned forward. “It’s also about developing their critical thinking skills. We need to teach them to question what they see and hear, to understand that not everything they come across is true or right.”

"And to be confident in their own beliefs," Mr. Chatterjee continued. “They ought to understand that being unique is acceptable and that they don't have to blend in with the pack.”

Michael gave a nod. “Without a doubt. It's about boosting their self-confidence and assisting them in realizing their value. They'll be less susceptible to bad influences if they have confidence in themselves and their decisions.”

Arpita developed a deep feeling of gratitude for the support of their friends. “We’re lucky that we are friends. It is good to see that our children are growing up in a community that values them and supports them. That makes a big difference.”

Sarah smiled warmly. “It really does. We will make sure that we keep on reinforcing those values every day and every time we interact.”

The two families continued their conversation till late in the evening. They exchanged their aspirations and anxieties, They discussed methods for raising confident and resilient children. They discussed the value of being present in their childrens' life. They thought of establishing boundaries, and keeping an eye on their online activity.

As the evening progressed, Mr. Chatterjee began to tell a tale from his own youth. Mr. Chatterjee started recalling a story about his own childhood. "My father always taught me that I was in charge of my own behavior, irrespective of whatever other people did. He believed that one should always act morally even if there was no one else around. He said it was a sign of integrity.'

Michael nodded. "That's amazing, a powerful message indeed.This is the lesson that we must teach our children. They must realize the importance of what they do. They must understand that they have the ability to have a positive influence."

Arpita added, "And they need to feel supported. They should know that we're here for them, no matter what. That they can come to us with anything, without fear of judgment."

Sarah agreed. "That is very significant. Children who experience safety and support at home will be more capable of managing the difficulties they may encounter outside.

Both families departed that evening on a positive note. They were determined to raise their children together, with love, understanding, and support for one another. Even though they understood it would not be an easy task in today's environment.

As they were ready to leave, Mr. Chatterjee turned towards Michael and Sarah. "I thank you for a lovely evening. These discussions are really important. They help us remember that we're not doing this alone."

Michael smiled. "We're all in this together. And as long as we keep talking and supporting each other, we'll be okay."

Arpita hugged Sarah. "Thank you for being such good friends. It means a lot to us."

Sarah returned the hug. "We feel the same way. We're lucky to have you."

The Chatterjees experienced a profound sense of calm as they strolled home together. They understood that parents cannot always protect their children from all bad influences. However, they could guide and encourage them. They could render support to them when they face difficulties growing up. And they felt prepared to take on everything that came their way because they had friends like. Petersons.

The Petersons and the Chatterjees were eager to know about their kids' development. They wanted to discuss their experiences with other parents. Hence they showed up at the school for the Parent-Teacher Conference (PTC). The school courtyard looked lively with noise of the conversation of parents as they engaged in small talk and exchanged information. The Petersons and Chatterjees recognized a number of familiar faces from their neighborhood.

Mr. Chatterjee: "Hey Michael, Sarah! How are you two? It's good to see you here."

Michael: "Hello Mr. Chatterjee, Arpita. We're doing well, thanks. How about you?"

Arpita: "We're good, thank you. Excited to hear how the kids are doing. And maybe a bit nervous too, as always."

Sarah: "Yes, I am also feeling a bit anxious. Yet I am excited too. You know, I'm going through a mix of both. But it's great to connect with other parents and share experiences. Shall we move inside?"

The group entered the main hall of the school, where teachers were waiting to meet parents at their respective tables. They sat in a circle with a few other parents in a more relaxed atmosphere. After a few introductions and brief updates from the teachers, the parents made themselves comfortable.

Mrs. Thompson, another parent, started the discussion. "It's great to see so many of us here. I think these meetings are crucial not just for understanding our children's academic progress but also for sharing our thoughts on their overall development."

Michael showed his consent. "Absolutely. We were just discussing how crucial it is to teach our children morals. We're all really passionate about it."

Mr. Chatterjee agreed to whatever Michael said. "Yes, values like equality and respect for all. It's essential that our children understand that everyone has equal value, regardless of their background."

Mrs. Thompson nodded."I agree. And it's not just about telling them; we need to model that behavior ourselves. Kids learn a lot by observing us."

Arpita agreed. "That's true. We try to demonstrate respect in all our interactions. It's important for children to see that in action, whether it's at home, in school, or in the community."

Sarah raised questions out of curiosity. "And what about self-conviction and confidence? How do you all encourage your children to believe in themselves?"

Michael added, "We want to provide our kids with independence so they can make independent decisions and grow from the results. It's about giving individuals the freedom to express their opinions and supporting them while they make decisions."

Mr Chatterjee said, "That's right. It's also critical to offer constructive criticism and encouraging words. Children gain confidence when they perceive that their efforts are valued."

Mrs. Thompson said, "Yes, and helping them set and pursue personal goals. Breaking down bigger goals into smaller, manageable steps can make a huge difference."

Arpita said with excitement."Celebrating milestones along the way is so important too. It keeps them motivated and teaches them the value of persistence and hard work."

Sarah shared her inputs, "Balancing personal goals with social responsibilities is another challenge. We want our children to be ambitious but also considerate of others."

Michael agreed with Sarah and presented his thoughts. "We've been encouraging our kids to think about the broader impact of their actions. It's about finding that balance between personal achievement and contributing positively to society."

Mrs. Thompson added to Michael's thoughts. She said,"Community service can be a great way to teach social responsibility. Volunteering as a family has been very rewarding for us."

Mr. Chatterjee nodded as he agreed with Mrs Thompson's "Absolutely. We've been involved in various community activities, and it's a fantastic way for the kids to see the impact of their actions firsthand."

Arpita shared her views "It also helps them develop empathy and kindness. Simple acts of helping a friend in need or sharing with peers can reinforce these values."

"How do you all approach discussions about social concerns and current events with your kids? We try to limit exposure to events they can't influence and focus on what they can."Sarah raised few more questions to clear her doubts.

Michael said, "We believe it's important to be informed but also to understand the limitations of our influence. We encourage our kids to focus on actionable steps and empowerment."

Mrs. Thompson was happy to know Michael's approach. "That's a great approach. It's easy to get overwhelmed by the news. Teaching kids to prioritize and act within their capacity is crucial."

"We also emphasize the importance of critical thinking and source verification. Understanding that different groups have different goals helps them navigate information better."Mr. Chatterjee added his thoughts about critical thinking.

Arpita raised her brows in doubt and to resolve her queries she asked,"And what about peer pressure or bullying? Have any of your children faced difficulties in this area?"

Sarah shared the incident of cyberbullying which her son had to face. "Unfortunately, yes. Our son Ethan has had some issues with cyberbullying recently. It's been tough, but we're working through it."

Michael talked about how they resolved the matter. "We've been having open conversations about it at home. It's important for children to feel safe discussing these issues with us."

Mr. Chatterjee said, "We've had our own experiences with bullying. It's crucial to build a strong support system at home so children know they're not alone."

Mrs. Thompson agreed. "Yes, and teaching them to stand up for themselves and others. Empathy and social duty go hand in hand."

Arpita shared her inputs."We've been trying to instill empathy in our children by encouraging them to understand and help others. It's about recognizing their role in the bigger picture."

Sarah was happy to hear that from Arpita. "That's wonderful. Empathy really is the foundation of social responsibility. When children understand themselves and their role, duty turns into opportunities."

As the discussion went on, parents shared their ideas and approaches. They talked about the difficulties in juggling homeschooling with formal schooling, as well as how to deal with the increasing use of technology and social media in their kids' life.

Michael asked parents, "We've been considering different schooling methods as well. What are your thoughts on homeschooling?"

Mr. Chatterjee expressed his views, "We've thought about it too. Learning is highly individual and personal. Each child has their own way of understanding and absorbing information.Group learning is important for social skills, but it's also vital to focus on individual needs. A balanced approach can be beneficial."

"Exactly. We need to understand that everyone has different learning styles. Finding what works best for each child is key.It's about providing options and letting children choose what suits them best. Supporting them in their choices is crucial." Mrs. Thompson shared her views.

Michael asked out of concern. "And what about the impact of social media and technology? How do you manage that with your children?"

Replied Mr. Chatterjee,"It's important to teach them about different types of relationships and the goals behind various online groups. Critical thinking is essential."

Mr Chatterjee continued,"Understanding source control and the intentions of different online entities can help them navigate the digital world safely."

Mrs. Thompson added,"We also emphasize the importance of real-life interactions. Balancing screen time with outdoor activities and face-to-face communication is vital."

Sarah excitedly shared her inputs as she agreed with Mrs Thompson. "Yes, introduction and presentation are crucial. We try to create an environment where our children feel welcome and included. Listening to their stories and showing genuine interest helps them feel valued. It's about fostering a sense of belonging."

"Belonging is a choice of accept and be accepted. It's about opening doors appropriately and creating opportunities for meaningful connections." Said Mr. Chatterjee.

Arpita added, "It's also important to help them understand their own role and responsibilities. When they understand themselves, they can better understand others."

"Absolutely, Mrs Chatterjee." Said Mrs. Thompson. She continued, "And that's where empathy comes in. Teaching them to see things from others' perspectives fosters understanding and cooperation."

Sarah firmly talked about a strong foundation that can nurture children. "It's all about building a strong foundation at home. When children feel supported and understood, they're more likely to thrive in society."

The parents felt a connection as they proceeded to share their thoughts and experiences. The parents understood that cooperation and exchange of thoughts and ideas are essential to develop a nurturing environment for children.By the time the evening came to an end, parents had a better knowledge of the principles they wished to teach their kids as well as how to get there.

Each parent felt more prepared to handle the difficulties of parenting children in a complicated world after the enlightening talk. They knew that by working together and sharing their insights, they will be able to develop an atmosphere where children can learn and flourish.

As Parent-Teacher Conferences (PTC), progressed, the topic of discussion quickly turned to how to balance personal beliefs with that of the outside world.

Mr. Peterson started the conversation. "Even if we try hard to push values in our children,sometimes, it's challenging. It becomes difficult to balance our values with the values they encounter outside."

Mrs. Chatterjee also agreed to whatever Michael said. "I totally agree. It's important to teach our children to be true to their own beliefs. However, they also need to be open-minded and respectful of others."

Mrs. White, another parent, chimed in. "We face the same challenge. Our daughter has strong opinions, but we want her to learn how to navigate situations where others might not share her views."

The ever-considerate Mr. Chatterjee continued, saying, "I think the most important thing is to teach children to understand and appreciate their own beliefs first. If they do so, they will be able to appreciate others and develop a strong sense of self."

Mrs. Peterson smiled. "That's true. But it's also about teaching them when to stand firm and when to be flexible."

The conversation flowed naturally as they shared stories and insights.

Mr. Peterson shared an example. "Our son, Ethan, loves debating. He's passionate about certain topics. We've encouraged him to find common ground with his peers rather than just arguing his point."

Mrs. White nodded. "That's a good approach. It helps them know that if their convictions are important, so are the perspectives of others."

Mrs. Chatterjee agreed. "Exactly. When Raj was younger, he struggled with this. But over time, he's learned to listen first and then speak. It's made a huge difference."

Mr. Chatterjee, always the philosopher, said, "One thing we must remember is that every process takes its own times. It's important to be patient with our children and with ourselves."

Mrs. Peterson added, "Yes, and sometimes the right time to address certain issues isn't immediately obvious. We've learned to give our children space and time to process things on their own."

Mr. White, who had been listening quietly, spoke up. "I think knowing when to step back is also crucial. We can guide them, but we must let them find their own path."

Mrs. Chatterjee smiled. "That's true. And sometimes, if there's too much resistance, it's better to pause and revisit the issue later."

The conversation turned to practical strategies.

Mrs. Peterson suggested, “We try to expose our children to diverse viewpoints. Books, travel, and even conversations like this one help them see the world from different angles.”

Mrs. White agreed. “ I heard Mr Chatterjee and Mr Peterson discuss encouraging critical thinking and teaching empathy. We too practice that with our children. We want our children to question things, to understand why they believe what they do.”

Mr. Chatterjee added, “We also emphasize empathy. Understanding others’ perspectives is essential. We’ve found that volunteering and community service help build this empathy.”

Mrs. Peterson looked thoughtful. “It is important that our children express their thoughts and feelings without fear of judgment.”

Mr. Peterson concluded, “Ultimately, it’s about balance. Balancing our guidance with their independence, our values with their experiences.”

The conference came to an end when the school bell rang. The parents got up. They were overwhelmed by the feeling of unity and shared purpose.

"You know, these talks are so valuable," Mrs. Chatterjee said to Sarah Peterson as they left. “They are a reminder that we are not alone in this journey.”

Sarah smiled. “Without a doubt. It is clear that although our approaches are different, yet our objectives remain the same. We all want our children to become all rounder. We want them to be considerate, and empathetic adults.

After they returned home, the Petersons and the Chatterjees remembered the conversations of the day.
They talked to their children about what they had learned. They emphasized the importance of understanding and balancing their convictions with the world around them.

Both families deliberately tried to put the techniques they had discussed into practice in the following weeks. They pushed their kids to ask questions, think critically, and develop empathy. By giving their kids more chances to engage with various groups, they promoted an atmosphere of respect and understanding between people.

As a result, the kids started to move through their environment with more assurance. They discovered how to appreciate other people's beliefs while proudly clinging to their own. They recognized that their experience was distinct, but that they were part of a larger humanity.

The Chatterjees and Petersons became closer and closer. They kept talking about their experiences, helping and learning from one another. They were dedicated to the process of reconciling their inner beliefs with the outer world, even though they understood it would take time.

Ultimately, it was about building a community where people with diverse ideas could live in harmony rather than just trying to strike a balance between them. It was about instilling in their kids the value of being authentic while celebrating global variety. Above all, it was about realizing that the trip was just as significant as the end point.

The Chatterjees and the Petersons were happy that they are traveling down the correct path together.

Chapter 9 - The Shy Superhero

The Petersons sat around their kitchen table, their faces etched with concern. Ben, their youngest son, had always been shy. His reluctance to participate in class plays was now causing him to withdraw even more. Sarah, his mother, looked at her husband, Michael, with worry.

"Michael, we need to do something about Ben. He's been refraining himself from school activities, and it's getting worse," Sarah said, her voice trembling slightly.

Michael nodded. "I know, Sarah. He's not like Ethan. He's more sensitive and introverted. But we can't let him continue like this."

Ethan, their older son, who was always supportive of his younger brother, sat nearby. He looked up from his homework and joined the conversation. "Maybe he needs a change. A new environment might help him open up."

The idea of changing schools had been on their minds. Ben appeared to be an excellent fit for the school they had thought of. It was just a little away from their house. However, it was intimidating to consider sending him to a new school. Ben's parents didn't want to press too hard because he was reluctant.

Sarah took a deep breath. "I believe we should clarify to him the distinction between the feelings and emotions. He must realize that although his emotions are real, he can find new ways to communicate them.

That evening, they decided to talk to Ben. They found him in his room, drawing quietly. Sarah sat down next to him on his bed.

“Ben, I want to have a serious conversation. It's about something important," she said softly. “It has come to our attention that you are finding it difficult to engage in school-related activities. We wish to assist you in realizing that feeling timid or afraid is acceptable.”

Ben was unsure. He looked up at his mother, his eyes wide open. “But I don’t feel it that way, Mom. It makes me feel different.”

Michael joined them, sitting on the other side of Ben. “Ben, feelings are our way of connecting with the universe. They protect us and help us understand what’s going on around us. On the other hand emotions are the way we express those feelings. Sometimes, it becomes difficult to find the right words or the correct behavior to show what we’re feeling.”

Sarah nodded. “That’s right, Ben. Feelings are important to listen to. They tell us what we need. But we can find different ways to express them. For some people, that might be through talking. For others, it could be through painting, drawing, or even playing."

Ben thought for a moment. "So, it's okay to feel scared about the school play?"

"Yes, absolutely," Michael said. "But we can find ways for you to express that fear. Maybe you can draw how you feel, or write a story about it. The important thing is to find tools that work for you."

Despite their efforts to comfort Ben, he remained hesitant about participating in school activities. Michael and Sarah continued to discuss about the idea of moving him to a new school.

One evening, while they were sitting together in their living room, Sarah stated, "We need to consider what's best for Ben."
Perhaps a new school with a different approach will make him feel more at ease."

Michael agreed. "At present it may seem to be a big step. However, if it can help him grow emotionally and socially, I think it's worth it. We should also make sure the new school has a good support system for him."

Ethan, who was listening from the doorway, walked in and sat down with them. "I'll help Ben. I'll make sure he feels comfortable and safe. Maybe having me around will make the transition easier."

Discussing the Move with Ben

The next day, they sat down with Ben to talk about the possibility of changing schools.

"Sarah began, "Ben, we've been thinking about something. We think that you would benefit from switching to a new school. It's a place where you can make new friends. You can even have different experiences.

Ben looked anxious. “But what about Ethan? Will he be there?”

Michael smiled. “Yes, Ethan will be there with you. He wants to help you through this change.”

Ethan put his hand around Ben’s shoulder to comfort him. “Don't worry. I’ll be with you on each and every step, Ben. We can do this together.”

Ben took a deep breath. “Okay. I am ready to give it a try.”

The Petersons got ready to move to the new school as the days went by. They went to the school and had a word with the instructors. They made sure Ben was at ease in his new surroundings.

One afternoon as Ben was putting his school bag together, he glanced up at his mother. "What if I don't fit in, Mom? What will happen if I'm disliked by the other kids?

Sarah knelt down to his level. "Ben, it's normal to feel worried about that. But remember what we talked about. You have feelings, and that's okay. You can express them in different ways. And you'll have Ethan with you. Plus, you're a wonderful person, and I'm sure you'll make new friends."

It was the first day of the new school. Out of his nervousness, Ben made sure to hold his brother's hand tightly as they entered the building.

The first day at the new school arrived. Ben was nervous, but he held his brother's hand tightly as they walked into the building. Ethan was by his side, offering constant support.

Their new teacher, Mrs. Williams, greeted them warmly. "Welcome, Ben. We're so happy to have you here."

Throughout the day, Ben found that the new environment was more welcoming than he had anticipated. The teachers were understanding, and the other students were friendly. With Ethan by his side, he felt a sense of security.

Over the next few weeks, Ben slowly began to adjust to his new school. He found comfort in expressing his feelings through drawing and writing. Mrs. Williams asked him to present his work to the class after noticing his talent.

One day, Ben was asked to read one of his stories aloud to the class by Mrs. Williams. Ben was apprehensive at first, but he agreed after hearing Ethan's encouragement.

His hands began to shake, when he stood in front of his peers. But when he started to read. Gradually, he saw a rise in his confidence. The students listened attentively, and they cheered when he was done.

Mrs. Williams smiled. “That was wonderful, Ben. Thank you for sharing.”

Ben beamed with pride. For the first time, he felt that he was a part of that school.

At home, the Petersons continued to have open conversations about feelings and emotions. They wanted to ensure that Ben understood the importance of emotional growth.

“Ben, how do you feel about your new school?” Sarah asked one evening.

Ben thought for a moment. “I like it. Though I still get nervous sometimes, but I’m learning. I am learning to express my feelings. Mrs. Williams really helps.”

"That's wonderful to hear, Ben," Michael continued. Remind yourself that it's acceptable to feel differently. The way you convey them matters. And you're working really hard at it.

Ethan added, "Ben, I'm proud of you. You're truly being more transparent and showcasing your abilities to everyone.

Ben smiled. "Thanks, Ethan. I couldn't have done it without you."

As the family continued to support Ben, they reflected on their own experiences with emotional growth. Michael shared a story about his own childhood.

"When I was your age, Ben, I also had trouble expressing my feelings.I had my feelings were different from everyone else. However, I eventually discovered how to express myself on my own. Even though it's not always simple, it's crucial to persevere."

Sarah nodded. "In our family, we have often faced problems with expression. We had difficulties accepting that not everyone has their way of looking at things; that they don't see things the same way. We need to know that it's easy to get frustrated. However, we need to remember that everyone has their own perspective."

Ben continued to progress as he got the support of his family and his new school. He had become more confident in expressing his feelings and emotions. He discovered that drawing and writing were powerful tools for him to communicate his inner world.

One evening, as the Petersons gathered in the living room, Ben showed them a drawing he had made. It depicted a colorful landscape with a small figure standing in the middle.

"This is me," Ben explained. ""I'm in the center, and everything that surrounds me is vibrant and luminous. I feel like I'm able to express myself.

Sarah hugged him. "That's beautiful, Ben. We're so proud of you."

It was a difficult road to assist Ben get over his reserved nature and reluctance to take part in school activities. It requires tolerance, comprehension, and an openness to trying out various emotional expression techniques. The Petersons discovered that they could assist Ben's emotional development by emphasizing the value of emotions and giving him the appropriate means of expressing them.

Through their experiences, they also realized the importance of balancing personal convictions with the outside world. They were aware that different processes require different amounts of time. It is a wise decision to occasionally pause to address problems later, as and when required.

Ben's transition to a new school and his personal growth ultimately strengthened the Peterson family's bond. They knew that the road to emotional development was not over, so they kept encouraging one another. Most importantly, they discovered that they could support one another through life's obstacles if they had love, tolerance, and understanding for one another.

The Petersons and the Chatterjees often reflected on their shared experiences. They wanted to develop empathy, respect, in their children. They wanted to cultivate emotional resilience. As they knew children like Ben, were growing up in a very complex world. They disired to prepare them for whatever challenges lay ahead.

****

One Saturday evening, the Chatterjee and the Peterson families gathered for their regular weekend get-together. The kids played in the backyard. There was a light breeze blowing and the rustling of the leaves could be heard clearly on that peaceful evening. Michael and Mr. Chatterjee were enjoying their drinks while sitting on the patio's edge and taking in the calm surroundings.

Mr. Chatterjee broke the cozy silence, "Michael, I have been intending to ask you something." Sarah told me that Ben has been feeling a lot better lately.

“Michael,” Mr. Chatterjee began, breaking the comfortable silence, “I've been meaning to ask you something. I heard from Sarah that

Ben has been doing much better lately. How did you help him overcome his shyness?"

Michael smiled, setting his drink down. "Though difficult, yet, the trip was worthwhile. We saw Ben's timidity from the beginning, since the time he had started schooling. Lately it had become more obvious. He was reticent to engage in social situations. He frequently kept himself away from school gatherings.

Mr. Chatterjee nodded, his expression thoughtful. "I understand. Arpita and I have noticed similar traits in our son Raj at times. So, what did you do?"

Michael leaned back, gathering his thoughts. "Firstly, it was important to acknowledge Ben's emotions. We came to see that his shyness was just a natural aspect of who he was and nothing to be ashamed of. We discussed his emotions with him and let him know that it's normal to feel terrified or nervous. These emotions are common and everyone has them occasionally."

"That's true," Mr. Chatterjee agreed. "But how did you help him express those feelings?"

"We found that Ben needed tools to express himself," Michael continued. ""Sarah and I encouraged him to express himself through writing and painting. We purchased a sketchbook and some colored pencils for Ben. As he fond of drawing. We encouraged him to draw what he was feeling whenever he felt overwhelmed. He eventually came to regard drawing as a secure means of expressing his feelings."

Mr. Chatterjee's curiosity glowed in his eyes. "It's a really good idea. He can express himself without feeling compelled to talk in front of people."

"Exactly," Michael said, smiling. "We also decided to change his school environment. His previous school wasn't a good fit for him. We found a smaller school with a more supportive environment. The teachers there were more attentive to each child's needs, and that made a huge difference for Ben."

"How did he handle the transition?" Mr. Chatterjee asked.

Michael paused, remembering those initial days. "At first we found it to be a challenging task. Ben was not ready for the change. Hence he was scared. However, we made sure he knew he wasn't alone.

His older brother, Ethan, was a huge support. Having Ethan at the same school helped Ben feel more secure. We also worked closely with his new teachers to ensure they understood his needs."

Mr. Chatterjee smiled, appreciating the thoughtful approach. "It sounds like a lot of effort, but clearly, it paid off."

"It did," Michael said. "I believe it's all about patience and understanding. We stood by him for every step he took. We celebrated his small victories and encouraged him to take new steps. Over time, Ben started participating more in class. He has even made a few friends. Seeing him open up and gain confidence was incredibly rewarding."

Mr. Chatterjee nodded, deep in thought. "Thank you for sharing this, Michael. It gives me some ideas for Raj. I think we can try some of these strategies to help him with his own challenges."

Michael patted Mr. Chatterjee's shoulder. "Anytime. We're all together in this, raising our kids to be the best they can be. We should not forget that every child is different. What worked for Ben might need some adjustments for Raj, but with patience and love, I'm sure you'll find the right way."

The two men sat in comfortable silence for a moment, watching their children play and feeling grateful for the shared journey of parenthood.

*****

The following week, the school organized a parenting session. Both the Chatterjee and Peterson families decided to attend. The session promised to be informative and provide valuable insights into raising children in today's world. The parents were eager to learn and share their experiences.

As they arrived at the school, the hall was bustling with parents. There was a palpable sense of anticipation in the air. Michael and Sarah Peterson spotted the Chatterjees and waved them over. "Glad you could make it!" Michael greeted warmly.

"I wouldn't miss it," Mr. Chatterjee answered. "It's generally great to gain knowledge of new things."

The topic of why kids view their elders as role models was discussed at the start of the session. The speaker—a child psychologist—explained that kids pick up knowledge from seeing the adults in their environment. She stated, "People learn from each other."

Sarah nodded thoughtfully. "It's true," she whispered to Arpita. "Our actions speak louder than words."

Arpita agreed. "Yes, and it reminds us how important it is to set a good example."

The session then moved on to discuss signs that children exhibit when they are struggling. The psychologist explained that children often show clear signs of distress. "They may feel disconnected from the community. They find it difficult to see nuances and express themselves. Sometimes, they refrain from sharing their worldview with those around them."

Michael glanced at Ben, who was sitting quietly beside him. He remembered the times when Ben had struggled to express his feelings. The signs had been there, but they were subtle. "It's important to be observant," he thought.

The speaker continued, "When children struggle, they may withdraw or show a lack of interest in activities they once enjoyed. It's crucial for parents to notice these changes and address them promptly."

Mr. Chatterjee whispered to Michael, "This reminds me of what we discussed about Ben last week. Recognizing these signs early is so important."

Michael nodded. "Absolutely. It's all about being present and attentive."

During a break, the parents mingled and shared their experiences. Michael and Sarah found themselves talking to a group of parents about the importance of being role models. "Our children look up to us," Sarah said. "They see how we handle challenges and how we treat others. We need to be mindful of our actions."

Arpita joined in, "And it's not just about big gestures. It's about making small moves, everyday. These things make a difference. The way we speak to them, the way we listen, and the way we show empathy."

One parent asked, "What should one do when they notice their child struggling?"

Michael replied, "We create a space for them to express their feelings,where they feel safe. We use art and writing as outlets for Ben. It helps him communicate his emotions in a non-verbal way."

Another parent shared, "My daughter has been having trouble in school. I think I need to pay more attention to her signs."

Mr. Chatterjee added, "It's about knowing and understanding their perspective. It may happen that they don't have the words to express their feelings. We need to be patient and supportive."

The session resumed with practical tips on helping children cope with struggles. The psychologist suggested maintaining open communication and being non-judgmental. "It is necessary to encourage your children to talk about their feelings. Validate their emotions. Let them know it's okay to feel upset or scared."

Michael thought about how they had supported Ben. It had taken time and patience, but they had made progress. He shared, "We found that involving Ben in activities he enjoys also helped. It gave him confidence and a sense of accomplishment."

Mr. Chatterjee agreed, "For Raj, we found that spending quality time together, even just talking or playing a game, made a big difference."

The session ended with a Q&A segment. Parents asked about various challenges, from academic pressure to social media influences. The psychologist stressed on the importance of keeping balance. "Children not only need guidance, but they also need space to grow. They learn on their own. As parents, we should provide that balance."

As they left the session, both families felt a renewed sense of purpose. They knew parenting was a continuous journey of learning and adapting. Michael turned to Mr. Chatterjee and said, "I think today's session was really insightful for all of us. Knowing we're not the only one in this, is really comforting.

Michael turned to Mr. Chatterjee, "I think we all got some great insights today. It's reassuring to know we're not alone in this."

"Absolutely," Mr. Chatterjee replied. "We're all trying our best. And these sessions help us become better parents."

Sarah added, "It's also comforting to share our experiences. We learn so much from each other."

Arpita nodded, "Yes, and it reminds us of the importance of community. We're all in this together."

Back home, the Petersons and the Chatterjees felt more equipped to support their children. They were determined to be the greatest role models they could be, Though they knew it wouldn't be simple. They were aware of how critical it was to pay attention to their kids' needs, offer assistance, and create an atmosphere that values empathy and open communication.

Chapter 10 - The Question of Why

Anika sat quietly at the dinner table. Her small fingers traced patterns on the surface. She had been thinking about this question for days. She had noticed differences at school and around the neighborhood. She saw how other families celebrated holidays and spoke different languages. It made her curious and a little confused.

Arpita was preparing dinner when Anika finally gathered the courage to ask."Mom, why are we here?" Her voice was soft and hesitant.

Arpita turned to her daughter, surprised by the question. She saw the uncertainty in Anika's eyes. Setting down the spoon, she knelt beside her. "What do you mean, sweetheart?" she asked politely.

Anika hesitated, biting her lip. "I mean, why are we here, in this country? Everyone is different. They talk about things I don't understand. Sometimes I feel out of place."

Arpita's heart ached. She hadn't realized how deeply Anika had been affected. She took her daughter in her arms, pulling her close. "Oh, Anika," her voice softened, "I didn't know you were feeling this way."

Anika's eyes were filled with tears. "My peers at school ask me about our festivals. They always question me why we speak a different language at home. I don't always know what to answer. It makes me feel different."

Arpita took a deep breath, feeling the weight of her daughter's emotions. "Anika, we came here in search of a better life." We wanted you to grow up in a secure environment. Our desire was to expose you to different experiences. We thought we would be able to provide you more chances. To feel differently is acceptable. Our language and customs define who we are."

Anika sniffled, wiping her tears. "But why can't we just be like everyone else?"

Arpita's eyes filled with tears too. "Being different isn't a bad thing, my love. It makes us special. We have our own beautiful culture and stories. And it's important to share them with others."

Anika nodded slowly, starting to understand. "I just want to fit in."

Arpita smiled warmly. "You will, in your own way. And we'll always be here to help you. You're not alone."

Anika hugged her mom tightly, feeling comforted by her words. Arpita held her daughter close, silently promising to help her navigate these feelings. They would face these challenges together, with love and understanding.

That weekend, Anika stayed in her room, feeling low. Arpita and Mr. Chatterjee knocked on her door, but there was no reply. Their worry grew.

“Is everything alright?” Mr. Chatterjee asked, concerned.

Arpita sighed, “A few days back, Anika asked why we are here. I think it’s bothering her more than we realized.”

After an hour, Anika emerged, her eyes red from crying. Arpita immediately went to her. “Anika, what’s the matter?”

Anika looked at her parents, her tone serious. “Why are we here?”

Arpita responded gently, “We talked about this, dear. We came to this country for a better life.”

Anika shook her head, tears welling up again. “No, Mom, not in this country. I mean, why are we on this Earth?”

Her parents were taken aback, but Mr. Chatterjee quickly composed himself. He knelt down to Anika’s level. “That's a big question, Anika. Everyone has questions about it occasionally. Our goals are to grow, learn, and impact the world. Every one of us is here for a reason. It's acceptable to be confused. We are here to assist you in finding your way.”

Anika nodded slowly, feeling the love and support of her parents, and began to feel a little better.

Mr. Chatterjee knelt down and looked Anika in the eyes. "We are all on our spiritual journey, Anika."

Anika furrowed her brow. "What does spirituality mean?"

"Spirituality is about the fervor of life," Mr. Chatterjee began. "It's what makes people act on Earth, giving them purpose and drive."

Anika tilted her head. "Is spirituality personal?"

Arpita nodded and joined in. "Yes, it is very personal. Think of it like your favorite color. Everyone has their own favorite color. As each color has its unique way to speak to them. Spirituality is similar. It's a personal journey and understanding that each person has about their place in the world."

Anika pondered this. "So, it's like how I love drawing while others might love playing music?"

"Exactly," Mr. Chatterjee said. "Just like you express yourself through your art, others find their expression through different activities that resonate with their spirit."

Arpita added, "Imagine yourself being a plant in the garden. Are you alone? Do you have other plants around? Isn't the garden filled with different plants?" She gave Anika some time to understand by herself. After some time Arpita continued, "Some of us are sunflowers, some are roses, and some are little jasmines. Each plant has its own way of growing towards the light. That's their own way of thriving. That's like our spiritual journey. Each of us finds our own path."

Anika's eyes lit up with understanding. "So, spirituality is about finding what makes us grow?"

Mr. Chatterjee smiled. "Yes, Anika. It's about finding what makes us grow. It is about knowing what makes us feel alive and connected to everything around us."

Anika then asked, "If that is the case, how can one know what their spiritual path is?"

"That's the beautiful part of the journey," Arpita said. "We explore, we experience different things, and we listen to what feels right in our hearts. It's a lifelong journey, an adventure."

Mr. Chatterjee added, "Sometimes, spirituality may involve connecting with others. As we connect to our family and friends. Sometimes it's about finding moments where we can quietly reflect. It's about having balance. It's different for everyone."

Anika nodded thoughtfully. “So, it’s okay if I don’t know my path yet?”

“"Unquestionably," Mr. Chatterjee answered. “You have plenty of time to discover what gives you a sense of fulfillment and connection because you are still young. We are here to support you along your journey at every turn.”

Arpita gave Anika a hug. “Spirituality are self-awareness, empathy, and love—for oneself as well as for others. It has to do with having compassion. It even entails making a unique contribution to the world's betterment and everyone's enjoyment of living in it.”

Anika hugged her mom tightly. She felt reassured. “Thank you, Mom and Dad. I think I understand a bit better now.”

Mr. Chatterjee smiled warmly. “And we’ll always be here to help you understand more as you grow. Just remember to keep asking questions and exploring the world around you.”

Anika felt a sense of peace. “I will. I promise.”

With that, the family felt a deeper connection, knowing they were all on their unique journeys, supporting and learning from each other along the way.

One evening, Arpita and Sarah thought of going out for a walk. They went to the local botanical garden and made themselves comfortable in a quiet corner. The garden was full of flowers with vibrant colours. The garden was full of fragrance because of these blooming flowers. It was just a small escape from their routine busy lives. It was the perfect place for an uninterrupted conversation.

Sarah could sense Arpita's thoughtful mood, she asked, "You seem to be worried. I feel you have a lot on your mind. Is everything alright?"

Arpita sighed. "It's just... There's been so much going on with Anika lately. She's been asking a lot of deep questions. Especially questions about spirituality and our purpose on this earth."

Sarah nodded, her face reflecting understanding and curiosity. "How did you handle it? It's too much for a young child to understand."

Arpita smiled faintly. "It is. Yet I also see a wonderful opportunity. It made me think a lot about how spiritual principles affect our roles as parents."

Sarah leaned in, intrigued. "How so?"

Arpita took a deep breath, organizing her thoughts. "The most important thing about spirituality is to remember why we chose to come to Earth. Each of us has a purpose, a unique journey. As parents, we have the privilege to be a part in our their journeys right from the beginning. It's our job to explain how the system on Earth works and to show them how amazing our bodies are and what possibilities our beliefs can offer."

Sarah's eyes widened. "That's a beautiful way to look at it. It makes parenting sound like a sacred duty."

Arpita nodded. "It really is. For example, I've been explaining to Anika how feelings and emotions are different. Feelings are like a built-in system that protects us, a way to listen to the universe. Emotions are how we express those feelings. By teaching her to understand this, I'm helping her navigate her own journey."

Sarah looked thoughtful. "I've never thought of it that way. How does that change how you parent day-to-day?"

"It means I try to be very present and mindful," Arpita explained. "When Anika asks questions, I don't just give her quick answers. I try to help her explore and understand. I want her to know that it's okay to have her own convictions, even if they're different from mine. It's about balance – helping her see the possibilities while respecting her unique path."

Sarah smiled. "I think that's wonderful. It must be challenging, though, especially when she asks such profound questions."

“It is,” Arpita admitted. “Just the other day, she asked why we are here, not just in this country but on Earth. It made me realize she is thinking too much about these issues. I had to explain that we all have different spiritual journeys. It is for our learning and development. As we all are different, so are our ways.”

Sarah’s face softened. “That’s such a deep conversation for a child. But it’s beautiful that you’re having it. It must give her a lot of comfort to know she can ask you anything.”

“I hope so,” Arpita said. “It’s important to me that she understands and feels safe. It’s about showing her through my actions and not just by answering her questions. If she sees me showing compassion and understanding, I think it will help her to learn to be that way too.”

Sarah nodded. “That makes a lot of sense. It’s like leading by example.”

“Exactly,” Arpita agreed. “Furthermore, it goes beyond the major issues. It's the little things we do every day. It is being tolerant with one another and ourselves too. It is about being kind to strangers, and finding happiness even in the little things we have in our life. Our children find out how to handle their own travels from all of these experiences.”

Sarah looked thoughtful. “I think I will learn a lot from that approach. Sometimes I get so caught up in the daily routine that I forget to look at the bigger picture.”

Arpita smiled. “We all do. But spirituality helps us remember that bigger picture. Spirituality is a reminder for us that every moment is an opportunity. It is a journey to teach and to learn. And that’s a powerful thing.”

Sarah reached out and held Arpita’s hand. “I am so grateful to you for sharing that with me. It’s given me a lot to think about.”

“I’m very happy to have a friend like you. I am at ease as I can share everything,” Arpita said, putting her back at rest. “Parenting is such a journey, where you can't travel alone. You friends who are traveling with you through it.” Sarah added.

The sun continued to warm their faces, as they sat back and sipped their tea. The understanding between them deepened. Both of them knew that the conversations they had with their children and each other were trying to shape their paths in profound ways. This was guiding them through the challenges and joys of parenthood.

Arpita’s thoughts drifted back to Anika’s question about being on Earth. She remembered how Mr. Chatterjee had explained spirituality to Anika. He had told her that spirituality is about the fervor of life, the drive that makes people act and find purpose. He had likened it to being different plants in a garden, each growing towards the light in their own way.

Arpita had added that spirituality is about love, compassion, and understanding. It's about being kind and making the world a better place in your unique way. Anika had understood a bit better then, but her questions had opened a door for deeper exploration.

Reflecting on this, Arpita realized that teaching spirituality and purpose was not just a one-time conversation but a continuous dialogue. It was about helping Anika and Ethan understand their feelings, find their own paths, and embrace their unique journeys.

Sarah's voice brought her back to the present. "You know, I think our kids are really lucky to have us as parents."

Arpita smiled. "I think we're lucky to have them too. They teach us just as much as we teach them."

Sarah laughed. "That's true. It's a never-ending learning process."

The evening became darker, they drank their tea and decided to talk more about it later. They both had a resurgence of purpose and a better comprehension of their parental responsibilities. parents were aware that parents were contributing to the creation of a better, more interconnected world by accepting their own spiritual journeys and providing loving, compassionate guidance for their kids. Over the weekend, further discussions and introspection took place.

As the evening grew darker, they finished their tea and promised to continue their conversation soon. They both had a resurgence of purpose and a better understanding of their parental responsibilities. They knew that they were contributing to make their children a better human. So that their children remain more interconnected to the world by accepting their own spiritual journey. They wanted to provide them loving, compassionate guidance.

The weekend passed with more conversations and reflections. When Monday came, Arpita felt a renewed sense of peace and readiness to face the challenges ahead. She was aware that with every inquiry Anika posed, they were all developing as a group, figuring out their own routes, and encouraging one another along the way. She came to see that this was the fundamental nature of parenting: providing guidance, education, and love at every turn.

Sarah and Arpita strolled through the park, enjoying their evening walk. The sun was setting, and it had covered the sky with a golden hue over the trees.

"Arpita," Sarah began, "how do you explain the idea of a higher force or purpose to the kids?"

Arpita smiled, "The higher power is within each of us, Sarah. It's our task to know and redeem it within ourselves."

Arpita elaborated, "It is an inner force guiding us through life. It is the core of our spirit, our inner source of strength and knowledge. We can find peace, clarity, and purpose by comprehending and using it. This enables us to face life's obstacles with grace and assurance."

Sarah nodded thoughtfully, "How do you help your children understand that?"

Arpita replied, "By teaching them the power of breathing and meditation. It's an important key to higher power. "It's a simple practice. However, it helps them connect with their inner selves. Whenever they feel stressed or confused, we take a moment to breathe deeply and find calmness. It's a way to make us realize that peace and strength are always within reach."

Sarah felt inspired. "I'll try that with my kids too. It's such a beautiful way to find balance and inner peace."

Sarah looked curious. "Can you explain more?"

Arpita took a deep breath. "Breathing helps us to become aware of the current moment. Clearness and serenity can be experienced when we pay attention to our breath."

Sarah thought for a moment. "So, it's about being aware of the now?"

"Exactly," Arpita said. "When children learn to focus on their breath, they become aware of their inner strength and purpose."

Sarah smiled. "That's beautiful. I'll try it with my kids."

Arpita nodded. "It takes practice, but it helps them understand that they have a special purpose. We each have a journey to discover that purpose."

As they continued their walk, the conversation deepened, with Sarah feeling inspired by Arpita's wisdom. The simple practice of breathing became a bridge to understanding the higher power within, helping their children grow with a sense of purpose and inner strength.

This conversation sparked a journey of exploration for Sarah and Arpita about the meaning of life and the importance of finding inner peace. As they continued their evening walks, they often discussed how to teach these values to their children.

Arpita shared stories from her own childhood days. She explained in detail the lessons her parents instilled in her. They taught her about the value of maintaining calmness and inner strength.

Sarah then talked about what she has experienced and how she tries to give her children a sense of direction.

Then Sarah added, "In Christianity, there's a strong emphasis on praying. My mother always said that prayer is our way of talking to God, sharing our hearts, and seeking guidance. She believed that through prayer, we find strength, peace, and a sense of connection with God."

She continued, "I have taught my children to visit the church every Sunday morning. They also pray before having their meals. It's a moment to give thanks and remember that we are not alone. These small practices help them feel connected to something greater."

Arpita was amazed at how well Sarah was teaching the importance of praying to her children. She added, "From what I know, praying is a way of connecting to God in both Christianity and Islamic practices. It's beautiful to see how different faiths find a common ground in prayer."

She further said, "While in Eastern countries, connecting to the higher power is often through meditation. Meditation helps calm the mind, reduce stress, and bring inner peace. It allows individuals to connect deeply with their inner selves and the universe, fostering spiritual growth and clarity."

Arpita added, "I have heard about another practice called Journeying."

Sarah looked curious and confused. "I haven't heard about it. Can you tell me more?"

Arpita explained, "There's a group of people called the Shaman. In Shamanic practice, journeying is very important. They believe they travel to different realms with the help of rhythmic sounds, like drums or flutes.

"When you go on a journey, you can choose which realm you want to explore. The middle world is our materialistic world. The upper world offers a perspective from the gods or higher beings. The underworld lets you connect with a different type of energy. This helps you become very stable on Earth. It's somewhat similar to the chakra theory in Ayurveda."

Sarah listened intently, fascinated by this new concept.

They began incorporating these lessons into their daily routines. Arpita taught her children simple breathing exercises. Whenever they felt stressed or overwhelmed, they paused, took deep breaths, and focused on the present moment. Over time, the children started to find comfort in this practice.

Sarah introduced moments of reflection at home. Each evening, she asked her children to share something they were grateful for. This helped them focus on the positive aspects of their day and appreciate the little things.

Through these small but meaningful steps, both families began to see a change. Their children became more aware of their feelings and learned to handle stress better. They started to understand that true strength comes from within and that finding inner peace is an important part of life.

In their own ways, Sarah and Arpita taught their children that the journey to discovering a higher purpose starts with understanding and nurturing the power within themselves. This shared journey brought their families closer, helping them grow together in harmony and peace.

Verses Kindler Publication

Verses Kindler Publication

Reach us through our website -
https://www.verseskindlerpublication.com/
For more information visit our Instagram or Facebook page.